Bond, the Bea
and My Year with

Bond, the Beatles and My Year with Marilyn

50 Years as a Movie Marketing Man

CHARLES "JERRY" JUROE

McFarland & Company, Inc., Publishers
Jefferson, North Carolina

LIBRARY OF CONGRESS CATALOGUING-IN-PUBLICATION DATA

Names: Juroe, Charles, author.
Title: Bond, the Beatles and my year with Marilyn : 50 years as a
   movie marketing man / Charles "Jerry" Juroe.
Description: Jefferson, North Carolina : McFarland & Company, Inc.,
   Publishers, 2018 | Includes index.
Identifiers: LCCN 2018027570 | ISBN 9781476675107 (softcover : acid
   free paper) ∞
Subjects: LCSH: Juroe, Charles. | Press agents—United States—Biography. |
   Motion picture actors and actresses—United States. | Motion pictures—
   United States—History. | Celebrities—United States—History.
Classification: LCC PN2287.J865 A3 2018 | DDC 659.2/9792092 [B] —dc23
LC record available at https://lccn.loc.gov/2018027570

BRITISH LIBRARY CATALOGUING DATA ARE AVAILABLE

ISBN (print) 978-1-4766-7510-7
ISBN (ebook) 978-1-4766-3399-2

Front cover: the author strikes an iconic James Bond pose with a prop
Walther PPK handgun in the 1980s (EON unit photographer
Keith Hamshire)

Printed in the United States of America

*McFarland & Company, Inc., Publishers
   Box 611, Jefferson, North Carolina 28640
      www.mcfarlandpub.com*

Acknowledgments

I am indebted

... to film historian and prolific Bond novelist Raymond Benson for correcting names, titles, facts, and dates that the brain of a nonagenarian screwed up!

... to Ajay Chowhudry and Andrew Lycett for their sage advice.

... to Angela Niblock, MBA, for making sense of my scribbling and lack of punctuation.

... to great Bond enthusiast Mark Cerulli, for not only his long friendship but his invaluable help on this project.

... finally to Doug Redenius, a friend for all seasons, a Bond aficionado extraordinaire, and ... without whom this book wouldn't exist.

Special thanks: Barbara Broccoli, Michael Wilson, Stephanie Wenborn, Meg Simmonds, Dave Worrall and Anders Frejdh.

Table of Contents

Preface

This is not a novel, biography, or, even in the normal sense, an autobiography. It is, at best, an extended memoir. This is not about me, though most certainly it is a first-person account. My life is not what is of interest—rather it's the incredible number of famous people from many walks of life whom I've interacted with in my nine decades of existence. If a young publicist learns his lessons early, he knows his value is in what he says, but almost never to be seen saying it. Be it on the set, in the dressing room, at lunch, or in the hotel suite, photographers are usually not there to record relatively private interactions. Hence hours spent over time with the likes of the Beatles, Audrey Hepburn, Grace Kelly, et al., rarely ends in visual coverage.

*   *   *

At the start of the 1990s when I retired as senior vice-president of one of legendary producer Cubby Broccoli's production companies for the making of the James Bond films, I gave much thought to my years of working around the world in the motion picture industry.

I realized that there were an incredible number of major personalities whom I had met and/or come to know, not just in my working life but even from my earlier years. There were also famous names whose careers made them household names.

During my retirement, I've lost count of those who have said, "You should write a book; there is so much you have to say about the famous people you have met."

Though I do understand that the uniqueness of my Gulliver's Travels in Hollywoodland and beyond might be of interest, I also find that reminiscing is a great way of killing time before time kills! My longevity unfortunately means that a very large number of those I mention have already signed options with the Big Studio Boss in the Sky. Roger Moore's death caused much reflection for me. If and when I might ever meet Roger or any of these personalities again, I hope they will know I have only told it like it was. There are countless others who have also been in the business of making, distributing, or promoting films who could write such a book, but my path along such a celebrity-filled Yellow Brick Road is somewhat unique in that it goes back to almost my first steps and just went on and on and on...

When You Look
upon a Star

If there is one word that captures the glamour and wonder of motion pictures it certainly would be STAR. Unfortunately, this description of a rare and usually beautiful creature has been lessened over the years. There was a time when there were only a precious few who truly could be so-called.

Today, an actor can be in but one scene with perhaps a line or two of dialogue and some newspaper or magazine will state that he or she "starred."

One must now use the superlatives "superstar" or "megastar" to describe a truly big name. Even Jesus Christ had to be so described in the Andrew Lloyd Webber/Tim Rice musical, so what the hey!

To those of earlier generations, a star is a star is a star, as Gertrude Stein might have said.

Close Encounters
of the Weird Kind

The First

"Weird" is described in the dictionary as "something uncanny, fantastic, mysterious, and strange." All those words can apply to events that took place for me in two small towns over three thousand miles apart, one on the West Coast of America and the other on its east. If I am a committed fatalist, the following three happenings will explain why! It is truly amazing that these events all came full circle in my later life.

The very first was with someone who was destined to become one of the biggest names in the history of the cinema and it took place when I was literally still a baby. The story follows: My father had been a career naval officer during World War I and in the immediate post-war years. He left the service to try life as a civilian in San Francisco, California, where I was born. One of his earliest jobs in the mid-twenties was selling forgery insurance, though the real money was made because of a relatively new invention, included with the policy, called a check-writer. This was a tabletop machine that imprinted numbers that were actually cut into the paper. Such a check could not be tampered with and was therefore forgery-proof. This was how he supported his young family and, fortunately, he did well at it.

One of his closest friends was a business associate and fellow salesman named Joe Maysuch, a very handsome man of Italian heritage. Joe was married to a most glamorous blonde named Bernice (known to one and all as Bunny). They were to remain together until his death in the nineties.

My first "star" involvement begins by explaining that Bunny had been married once before (little more than a child bride) to a pharmacist in the then sleepy little town of La Jolla, just north of San Diego. The pharmacist was named Peck and at this time they had a son named Eldred. If you've not already guessed where this is going, I should mention that Eldred's middle name was Gregory. In those days Eldred Gregory Peck was a student at a military school near Los Angeles. Bunny and Joe were usually "on the road,"

The author (far left) enjoying a day at the beach with family members including his mother (in back, wearing white hat) and a young Gregory Peck (far right). Gregory Peck's mother, "Bunny," is front row, center (author's collection).

often in company with my parents, so Greg spent most of his vacation time with his father. Often when my parents were away I would live with Joe and Bunny.

On one occasion when Greg was with his mother on a short school break, we were all together for a seaside holiday. I have no memory of that day and I know it had little impression on a twelve-year-old stuck with a bunch of adults and an infant.

A subsequent meeting took place once at his home in 1948. When I showed him the photos from that day that had miraculously survived the years he barely recalled it; however, he most certainly wanted copies, as he had never seen the pictures before.

There was never to be what could be described as a real friendship between us; small wonder, a star and a film company publicist/executive exist on different planets. For example, when I was number two in charge of publicity at the Universal Pictures' East Coast office in New York, we had a major world premiere of the film *MacArthur*, honoring the great military hero and which starred Greg in the title role. The gala was at Radio City Music Hall and would feature a parade of West Point cadets up Fifth Avenue.

Prior to that there was a major national press gathering at the Academy on the Hudson, some fifty miles north of the city. Peck flew in from California for the events and we were together for a few days. We reminisced about that much earlier time in our lives and how strange it was that we both went on to careers in the motion picture industry, albeit me in the lower echelons and he in his rarefied position as one of the greatest film stars of all time. I know this reality certainly reflected my thoughts and I am sure Greg felt the same way, although he never said or did anything to indicate this obvious fact of his eminent position in the pantheon of filmdom.

Joe and Bunny would always loom large in my life though time and distance would always be a problem in the continuing closeness of our relationship. We last met in San Francisco in the mid-eighties, a few years prior to Joe's death, when I was there on location for the Bond film *A View to a Kill*. My great feelings for Bunny continued and we did occasionally communicate until she passed away at over one hundred! She had lived her final years with her beloved son and his family at his Beverly Hills Estate.

Gregory Peck was one of but a handful of film stars who can truthfully have been called Hollywood royalty, and I almost certainly met him long, long before anyone else who ever worked on a film set!

The Second

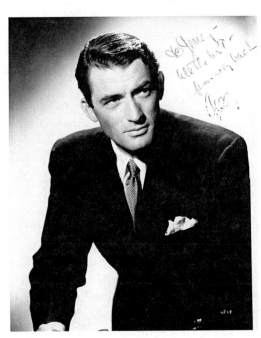

When I was a pre-teen I went to live for a couple of years with a sister of my mother in the small coastal town of Washington, North Carolina, at the mouth of the Pamlico River, just inland from Cape Hatteras.

My Aunt Katherine had married a local man from one of Washington's oldest families. They lived with their sons (my cousins) in a large wooden frame house not far from the one main street with its small cinema and shops. I spent two very happy years there, and my

Inscribed Gregory Peck studio portrait (author's collection).

7

best friend was a fellow grammar school student in the fifth and sixth grades named Murray Hamilton.

Murray lived about two blocks away from my aunt's home and we two boys were always together.

I particularly remember at one of the school entertainment activities when we did a tap dance (in those days called a buck-and-wing) wearing makeshift tuxedos with black cardboard top hats. It was truly a real life happening of one of those Andy Hardy "Let's put on a show!" moments so indicative of life in the thirties in small-town America.

Fate moves in mysterious ways. My little schoolmate and best friend Murray went on to a life on the New York stage, where he became a successful enough actor to play major parts in many Broadway shows, the most famous of which was certainly his being in the original company of Henry Fonda's *Mister Roberts*. He was not only one of the principal sailors but most importantly, the first understudy to David Wayne in the major role of Ensign Pulver. Murray took over the part when Wayne left for Hollywood after signing a contract with MGM. Jack Lemmon, who played Pulver in the Warner Bros. film version, became a star after winning an Oscar for this first role.

Murray's career never quite reached that level of stardom, but he did become a most successful working actor with a lengthy career on both stage and screen. Most often he played second lead as the "best friend" of the lead, be he a James Stewart, Paul Newman, or whomever.

His biggest film role was probably in the incredibly funny *If It's Tuesday It Must Be Belgium*, in which he starred in company with Suzanne Pleshette and a host of international names. His bit as the American tourist in the small Roman shoe shop with Vittorio De Sica is to me one of the funnier comedy sequences of language interplay ever put on sound film. Unfortunately, the picture was never a major hit, so not too many people saw this comedic gem. Most movie fans would probably recognize him as the mayor of the small Nantucket town terrified by the great white shark in the *Jaws* trilogy.

To me, however, his most famous part is the answer to a great trivia question. One of the most successful films of the sixties was *The Graduate*. The character played by Anne Bancroft, who, through her acting performance backed by the famous song by Simon and Garfunkel, became known throughout the movie-going world as the predatory Mrs. Robinson who seduced the young Dustin Hoffman in his film debut. So—"Who played the cuckolded Mr. Robinson?" The answer: my old school friend Murray! So as the iconic lyric might have been written, "Here's to you, MISTER Robinson."

8

I saw Murray a couple of times over the years. Once was in Chicago where he was starring on stage as the lead in the road company of *The Moon Is Blue*. The last time we met was when I was with Universal in New York, and my duties took me up to the location of the second *Jaws* being filmed in Hyannis Port, Massachusetts. I think the fact that I walked onto the set in company with producers Dick Zanuck and David Brown both impressed and surprised him. Murray Hamilton was not the only member of that small school class back in Washington, North Carolina, to have (as they say in show business) "made it."

The Third

The little cinema mentioned now becomes of importance because of something that took place in 1940, when I was back in Little Washington for

The author (left) in the Vatican gardens with Cecil B. DeMille (center) and longtime Paramount executive Luigi Luraschi (author's collection).

a summer. This event not only involved a parade but a gathering of all the current and recent students from Washington's grammar and high schools. I went along with my previous classmates, all of us now teenagers. We were there to welcome a world-famous film director who was a "son" of this tiny community. His Dutch forbears had lived there from the early 19th century, and at one time his grandfather had been the mayor following honorable service in the Confederate Army during the American Civil War (until he was captured by Union forces in a battle in the nearby town of Greenville). The family was originally named "de Mil," and this grandfather named William had married a local beauty named Margaret Blount-Hoyt. Their son, in turn, had two sons; the youngest was Cecil Blount de Mille, and he grew up to become, literally and figuratively, the founding father of Hollywood. He made his first film in a converted barn (still at Paramount). Hollywood's worldwide fame and its unique and unequalled place would not exist without the efforts and success of this man.

Many years later when I was working for him during the European premieres of Paramount's *The Ten Commandments* (discussed in a later chapter), I told him of that earlier meeting. He remembered being there because of the town's importance to him as the ancestral home of his family in America. He considered it little short of amazing that someone who also had family connections in Washington was years later working for him in the middle of Europe. This was compounded by the fact that I also had spent many working hours on the sets of his productions *The Greatest Show on Earth* and *The Ten Commandments* when I was a young publicist at the studio in the early fifties, though his personal publicist never let a studio publicist-type near him. The icing on this cake of coincidence was that one of my uncle's antecedents had actually worked in the mayor's office with his grandfather. We agreed it was, without question, a very small world.

When coupled with the events that took place some twenty years and a world war later, the three meetings mentioned from my childhood years can best be described as "weird."

Another coincidence of lesser importance, but still worthy of note, was when, as I was growing up, I decided to earn extra pocket money by selling, at five cents a copy, *Liberty* magazine in the neighborhood of our downtown San Francisco apartment. As I was only ten years of age, I still remember my mother following me at a distance to make sure no harm befell her "little angel." Anyway, I did very well and was one of the top kids in the Bay Area in sales, and as a result, our prize was a visit to the San Francisco branch office of Paramount Pictures for a private showing of the Gary Cooper hit *Lives of a Bengal Lancer*. It was my first time to see a film not showing in a cinema. Years later, I would spend quite a few working hours in that very building, both in and out of its screening room.

The Little Lieutenant

Stationed in America

When one looks back on a life, it is easy to pick out the times when the journey came to the "forks in the road." The track taken often determines mostly everything that follows. This first such happening for me came about when my parents, having more or less run out of family to help oversee my upbringing while they were away making a living, decided that the answer was to place me in a boarding school. I was duly enrolled at Castle Heights Military Academy in the small town of Lebanon in middle Tennessee, some thirty miles to the east of Nashville. I was enrolled in the seventh grade in September 1935. Two years later I moved up to the senior school for the four-year high school course. My father hoped that a military prep school might lead to my going to either of the American service academies (Annapolis or West Point). This was something that was not in my mind, although I did not have a clue as to what I wanted to do with my life at that young age. However, being in a military school was in no way a problem for me. Actually, I welcomed the whole idea, as it represented a form of continuity at the time.

My parents' decision put me on a path that dictated the rest of my life (though not quite in the way they intended). After six hard but carefree years, I graduated with my class in June 1941, almost six months to the day before Pearl Harbor put the United States into World War II. Those of us who were there the full four senior years had also been educated and trained in the ROTC (Reserve Officers Training Corps). Those years, plus a six-week summer course at an army base after the third year, meant that on reaching the age of twenty-one, a young man was eligible to become a Second lieutenant in the Army Infantry Reserve.

I went to Virginia after graduation and was enrolled at the Norfolk campus of the College of William and Mary, when the events of December 7 changed everything. All ROTC graduates eighteen years and upwards quickly received a letter from the Army Department asking about availability. As a result, I immediately applied for my commission. So, at the age of eighteen

A soldier and a sailor: with my father at the Top of the Mark in San Francisco, late 1942 (author's collection).

years and six months, I was suddenly in the army. This was in the middle of April 1942. To say that I looked like a Boy Scout was an overstatement; I had the appearance of a Cub Scout, someone barely in his teens. In many ways, this very youthful look cast a shadow of sorts over much of my army life, but this too was a factor that led me down that Yellow Brick Road to the golden city of Oz/Hollywood.

After finishing three months of intensive officer indoctrination training at Fort Benning, Georgia, I was sent to California to join the 134th Infantry Regiment of the 35th Division as a replacement officer. I much later learned that most of the young officers who entered the service east of the Mississippi were usually sent to West Coast units and those who had entered from the west of Mississippi were assigned to duty in the eastern part of the States. This is how I ended up in Southern California and was first exposed to the movie business. This was the second fork-in-the-road. Because I had entered the army from Virginia (even though I had been born in San Francisco and had spent more time in California than anywhere else), I was considered an "Easterner," so I was sent to Santa Barbara (north of Los Angeles) and billeted in a suite with five other officers at the famous "Country Club" in the Ojai

Valley, one of the most beautiful (and pre-war expensive) places to stay in Southern California. War is NOT always hell!

Because my superiors did not believe that I could lead troops, I was made sort of a glorified supernumerary. Every odd job there was for a young officer who was to be kept out of the way was mine, and this led to my first taste of Hollywood. A few months after arriving, I was sent down to Culver City to the studios of Metro-Goldwyn-Mayer, where I was to meet and accompany back to our troop areas two young actresses named Gloria DeHaven and June Allyson. They had been the female leads with star Van Johnson in a new film about to be released titled *Two Girls and a Sailor*. They were to visit selected military installations throughout Southern California, where the film would have various premieres. When my jeep arrived at the gate of the most famous studio of the day, I didn't realize that this was to be the first of literally thousands of such entrances to film studios around the globe.

A studio car took us up to Santa Barbara, and it was quite an experience for a young naïve teenager to suddenly find himself in the back of a Chrysler limousine with two very beautiful young actresses who probably considered me to be little more than a child (even though I had a gold bar on each shoulder). How was I to know how many hours I would be spending in the back of such limos with actors over my future working life? Though I tried to act professional about the whole thing, I am sure that both Gloria and June knew they were dealing with someone who had never been in such rarefied air before, but as it was *their* first promotional tour, it probably didn't matter.

In the mid-fifties, when June co-starred with Jimmy Stewart in *Strategic Air Command* at Paramount, I got to know her rather well. I almost told her of that wartime meeting, but decided that it was no longer relevant. It was a wise decision for me not to mention the earlier encounter as she was not as young and would not have wanted to be reminded of the obvious passage of time, however innocent the comment. That fact counts with all women, not just those who become actresses!

A few months later our unit was transferred to the big army camp at nearby San Luis Obispo. I was then assigned to Special Services (the army specification for entertainment, etc.) for our division. There was a first lieutenant in charge of such activity at the camp who was well known, having acted in a few films before and during the war—most notably *Johnny Eager*, for which he won an Academy Award for Best Supporting Actor. His name was Van Heflin and he was to go on to become a major star and enjoy a very successful career. When he starred in *My Son John* at Paramount, we reminisced about those war days at Camp San Luis Obispo.

Our principal duties were to organize and show the movies that were shipped up to the camp for screenings for the troops based there. These screenings and the rare three-day pass/leave were the high spots of the GIs' existence.

While I was there, a really big star came up to visit the camp as part of a tour of installations in California. I suddenly found myself having to assist Heflin in greeting one of the most famous and beautiful actresses of that time—Rita Hayworth. Somehow, I instinctively felt that if I was to have her confidence, while leading her around the camp, I was not to ask for an autograph or a photo. I can't say why I felt this way, but somehow it just struck me that it was not the thing to do. I was so right, but didn't really know it at the time. I was there to do a job, not to be a fan.

When Hayworth arrived in a transport plane at the camp's small airfield, Heflin had me along primarily to help our corporal take care of the baggage and the needs of the other people who came with her. She did have one woman, a sort of a maid/assistant/helper, who was pawned off on me while Heflin gave all his attention to Rita. I also went in advance of wherever she was to be around the gigantic installation with its thousands of troops.

Everything had to be set up by me so that the GIs could meet this great movie star with as little trouble as possible. She certainly carried off her visit to perfection, so, happily, it all went well. What is of interest is that when it was all over I had learned another lesson. I asked Heflin the obvious question, "Are you old friends with Rita?" (which I had never called her in person; it was always "Miss Hayworth"). He surprised me when he said they had never met before. He was at MGM and she was at Fox and they existed in more or less different worlds in Hollywood. I found this of very great interest, because it had seemed to me from their manner that they were old friends.

Another happening that reaffirmed this fact of star-to star relations came when my time in California ended in early 1944, and I was transferred to a soon-to-embark unit in Pennsylvania. This meant a long train ride across the United States, so another young officer and I duly left on the *Twentieth Century Limited* to go via Chicago to the East Coast. When we arrived in Des Moines, Iowa, there was a two-hour stop, so we travelers (military and civilian) went into the restaurant in the terminal. I found myself sitting next to the table of the well-known movie star Dana Andrews. At a certain point, in walked Jinx Falkenburg, a beautiful brunette with two or three people in her wake. One of the best-known models of the day, she had just started a movie career to much press acclaim. Andrews called out to her and they duly embraced amidst much hoopla. Her party joined his table, and I soon learned from their conversation that they too had never met before.

It's a fact that actors greet each other not only as equals, but as old friends. This "fellowship of exclusivity and celebrity" is a phenomenon that I know exists to this day. It is not unique to show business, but it is noticeable due to the recognition by the general public of people in the public eye.

I would meet Andrews again later at Paramount on *Elephant Walk*, but the coincidence factor again came into play when, in fifteen years' time, I would marry a beautiful English model/actress named Lynn Tracy, who was in a couple of scenes with him in the cult horror film *Night of the Demon*. More on that to come.

Stationed in Europe

I joined the 90th Division only three weeks before it sailed to England. My overseas duty took me from the UK to the invasion of Normandy, followed by combat across France, Germany, and into Czechoslovakia. After the Nazi surrender, we were assigned to southern Germany to begin the Army of Occupation. It was at this point in time that events took place that put me further on the road to a life in show business. Because of the impending invasion of Japan, which everyone knew to be inevitable, we European combat veterans were all very uneasy. We thought we would soon be transferred to fight in the Far East and were not going to survive two wars, so the ETO (European Theater of Operation) contained a bunch of very unhappy American campers at that time.

Amazingly enough, the army was very sensitive to this situation and instituted a very strong and continuing presence of civilian and army entertainers to keep the troops (particularly front-line types) relatively occupied and not be free to ruminate too much on what was going to happen when they got to the Far East. Because of the atomic bomb, this never came to pass, but in the early summer of 1945, no one in Europe was to know what the future held other than probable death somewhere in Japan.

The entertainment factor for the army units still based in Europe became a very high-profile endeavor. One fateful day a notice went out for the attention of junior officers (lieutenants and captains) from combat units who

Troops enjoy a jazz concert by the Major Glenn Miller Air Force Band in Germany after the war (author's collection).

wanted to volunteer to join Special Services and work with the entertainers. I immediately put my name forward and, happily, was selected. I am sure that this took place because even though I had survived the war, the people in command were very happy to have an excuse to get rid of this officer/baby of theirs. They obviously endorsed my request with singing praise of my singular abilities, and in short order I was transferred. The army thinking was that these liaison officers wearing combat infantry badges would not be considered typical rear echelon types, and the chance for a bust-up with front line veterans would be minimized. This was proved to be the correct approach. Over a period of a few months, I was on what could best be described as a revolving assignment. For example, I was with Major Glenn Miller's Air Force Orchestra for about three weeks. The famous band leader had been missing and presumed dead since mid–December, so the leaders on the bandstand were either Sergeant Jerry Gray or Sergeant Ray McKinley (both large figures in the civilian big band days). This was an extremely interesting assignment for I, like almost everyone else, was a fan of Miller's music. It was all very exciting for me to be around these great musicians who were doing such a marvelous job of entertaining day-in and day-out.

I was in awe of how often they had to perform. I worked very closely with the man who was actually in charge of everything that went on with the band. He was First Lieutenant Don Haynes, who had been Miller's civilian band manager. He wasn't an easy person to get along with, and in my humble opinion, seemed to think *he* was Miller. So as happy as I was with the assignment, I was equally pleased when I was transferred to a big show starring the famous comedian Jack Benny, the beautiful actress Ingrid Bergman, and Larry Adler (as well-known for his extreme left-wing politics as his phenomenal harmonica playing). It was my very first time being exposed to someone who thought that the sun rose and set in Joe Stalin and the Soviet Union. He never failed an opportunity to express this thought. My own reaction was that if he was that excited about communism, why didn't he move to Moscow? Anyway, this philosophy did have a bearing on me later on in oh-so-liberal Hollywood where I was not much in favor of those with a far-left point-of-view. On this score, I quickly learned to keep my mouth shut. It ain't easy being a minority.

Following Benny, I was assigned to Bob Hope's show. I really got along with Bob, which wasn't difficult as long as everything was under control and

With bandleaders Jerry Gray (left) and Ray McKinley (middle) during World War II (author's collection).

you did your job. The main concern in liaison work was to keep the inevitable problems to a minimum. Bob was an absolute delight to work with, and this short time with him certainly didn't hurt at all in my later years working with one of Paramount's biggest names. Another brief assignment found me with the International Sweethearts of Rhythm, the very professional all-woman big band. They were mostly black with two white New York women of the Jewish faith, a Puerto Rican, and a Chinese American. They were excellent musicians, and about half of them were exceptionally attractive. This was the only mixed-

Jack Benny fiddling for our troops after the war, accompanied by well-known American harmonica player Larry Adler (author's collection).

race entertainment unit never to have any redneck trouble from the biased white Southern soldiers to my knowledge.

I suddenly found myself in a rarefied situation. I now had sergeants and corporals galore to follow whatever was my wish or whim. The power word really came into being when I was sent to Paris to help select acts and entertainers for units to appear on the "circuit" (the American Army of Occupation in Germany and the Embarkation Areas of Southern France). It was at this time that a little boy truly became a man. Never again would any romantic period of my life compare, though there would be the odd day in future times in Hollywood, Paris, and London which came close! One of my most vivid recollections of that time was a meeting we had with one of the iconic showbiz figures of the 20th century, Marlene Dietrich, in her hotel room on the Champs-Élysées. We were there to discuss her possible tour of some of the camps. Unfortunately, for logistical reasons it didn't work out, but what a lesson for me in dealing with a world-famous personality. I tried not to show how in awe I was to be in her presence, but she treated me as a fellow professional, though a neophyte I certainly was.

I also met my first truly top line movie star when I had to discuss the

Bob Hope entertains the troops in Libya, 1950s (author's collection).

touring aspects of a possible all-soldier show starring Mickey Rooney. He had been assigned to produce and direct the extravaganza, but it never came to fruition. I always will remember when we first met; he called me "Jerry" and not "Lieutenant." Even the Miller musicians were more military than Sergeant Rooney! Of course, he was charm personified, and few have ever come close to his overwhelming personality and talent. And I learned there were very few WACs (Women's Army Corps) stationed at Hotel California on the Rue Berri whose eyes didn't light up when the diminutive Romeo's name was mentioned.

No college or university could ever compare to the importance of this education I received courtesy of Uncle Sam. All I knew was that *this* was what I wanted to do with my life and that somehow I would make it happen. That is precisely how it worked out.

An offshoot of this time was almost of equal importance to my future endeavors, although it didn't seem important at the time. I had my first experience with the media while in Paris. I encountered many of the U.S. press correspondents still in Europe prior to their going to the Pacific or back to

Eddie Fisher (left) and Bob Hope at a USO show at U.S. Airbase Wheelus, Libya, 1950s (author's collection).

the States. I am talking about the crème de la crème temporarily staying at the Hotel Scribe just down the Rue de la Paix from the Place de L'Opera where our Special Services headquarters were located.

Over a short time, I briefly met, among others, Ernest Hemingway, Robert Capa, Bill Maudlin, and Margaret Bourke-White. When you are around journalists and photographers of that ilk you quickly learned exactly how to interact with the most demanding and difficult.

As I went through my life dealing with the media, I likened myself to the Steinway piano with the journalist being the master musician who thought he was playing me. However, the trick was in getting from him the precise notes and music that *I* (the piano) wanted. Not easy to accomplish, but an ability that, once learned, became one of the keys (no pun intended) to the success of anyone in the public relations field of the entertainment industry.

In southern Germany after the war, 1945 (author's collection).

San Francisco "University"

Freshman Years

When I left the army in October of 1945, I went to San Francisco, where my mother was awaiting my father's return from his navy duty in the South Pacific. I had to make a living and I was in no mind to return to a university. All I knew was that I wanted to do anything that was in some way part of show business.

I first got a part-time job with a small distribution company releasing foreign films at its own small cinemas. The pay was almost non-existent, but it was a start. My main duties were taking stills (photos) and press releases around to the four main newspapers, two morning and two afternoon. In those days, the term for this was "planting" and I duly "planted" for about four months. Crazy as it may be, two of the pictures released during this short time were to become classics. One was the British duo Michael Powell and Emeric Pressburger's *The Red Shoes*, and the other the Jean Cocteau French masterpiece, *Beauty and the Beast*.

Meanwhile, my father returned and, after discharge, went into partnership with his old friend Joe Maysuch, but they were both too motivated to be the number one so they soon parted as the best of friends. After my parents left for Virginia, Joe offered me a job that fit in perfectly with my "film career." If I sold a check-writer, I got a commission, so it was up to me to flog them when I wasn't needed to work on the foreign film distribution. Everyone was happy and soon I was clearing about $100 a week with Joe, but he knew my heart wasn't in it as I kept trying to connect with one of the big cinema chains in the Bay Area. Eventually I was able to join (at a small percentage of my earnings with Joe) the giant Fox West Coast Theaters Corp. as an assistant manager in one of their small cinemas in one of the poorer districts of the city. After some months, I was transferred to the big Warfield Theater on Market Street, and then was later offered an opportunity to start in a very junior position in the company's publicity and advertising department because of the "experience" I had gained in the press department (just me) at the foreign film company.

It was during this period of my civilian career that I first professionally worked with personalities. It was the habit then for the studios in Los Angeles, some 500 miles down the coast, to promote many of their films in San Francisco. The first "stars" that I worked with were on an Eagle-Lion picture titled *He Walked by Night*. This film was not very important, but I do remember one player was a marvelous actor named Richard Basehart. The other was Scott Brady. I accompanied them as they went around meeting with the press. I much preferred when it was at lunch, as it meant a free meal! There were also appearances at the many radio stations or in their luxurious suite at the St. Francis Hotel.

Marie Wilson was among others I remember. These were not really big names, but it was certainly a good grounding for me in dealing with actors and their foibles. Wilson, a very bright and bubbly comedienne, was promoting *My Friend Irma*, which featured the young comedy team of Dean Martin and Jerry Lewis. Unfortunately, they were not along, but she was the star, whereas they were "just" a successful nightclub act appearing in their first film!

Another visit was the first promotional tour of a very young John Barrymore, Jr. (John Drew Barrymore), for his first film. It was fun to be the older man for once. All he was interested in was sex and where to find it. A generation later his daughter, Drew, became one of the world's sex symbols. Oh well, the carousel goes round and round!

One of my major learning experiences from that time was when David O. Selznick, the legendary producer of *Gone with the Wind* and *Rebecca* (the latter being the first Hollywood film for Alfred Hitchcock and the second for Laurence Olivier), came up with some of his actors for the sneak preview of *Duel in the Sun*, one of the biggest epic western films of the period. Among the stars there were Jennifer Jones (soon to be Mrs. Selznick) and Joseph Cotten. This was very important for me, as it was the first time I was exposed to a big Hollywood producer/studio head and his publicity machine. This experience only reinforced my certainty that this was what I wanted my life's work to be. I really learned a lot from everyone who was involved with Selznick, who was about as famous and successful as one could be. How was I to guess that some ten years later in London, England, I would become good friends with his eldest son Jeffrey, whose mother Irene was the daughter of Louis B. Mayer, no less.

Ironically the biggest star of *Duel in the Sun* was Gregory Peck, but he was not there; he was working on location. I was almost as upset as his mother, Bunny.

During the war I had found (looted) a small medallion from Lourdes commemorating Bernadette, the French peasant girl who observed the presence of the Virgin Mary in a cave near her home. I was so impressed with Jones' earlier performance in *The Song of Bernadette* that I gave it to her as a token of my esteem. It was possibly the only thing I ever did as a "fan." To my surprise, she gave me a signed autographed picture, which I kept, even though later on I came to abhor fan letters and the sending out of signed photos when I was briefly in charge of the fan mail department at Paramount in my early days in its publicity department.

A great tragedy befell San Francisco around this time when a major conflagration in the industrial area claimed the lives of some half-a-dozen firefighters. A giant charity performance for the widows and their families was arranged at the three thousand-seat flagship cinema Fox Theater, and I was one of the team assigned to promote the event and help coordinate the show.

A lot of names were involved, but two deserve mention. Frank Sinatra, post–MGM stardom and pre–Oscar glory, was the headliner, and a man every bit as difficult as reported. I remember thinking, "If he is like this now, just imagine what it must have been like when he was the singing idol of American womanhood!" I was to learn how demanding he could be first hand many years later when United Artists released *The Manchurian Candidate*.

The other performer of note was the iconic radio and movie star Edgar Bergen, certainly the best-known ventriloquist of all time. Backstage at the end of the show, I helped Bergen pack up his two famous dummies, Charlie McCarthy and Mortimer Snerd. To have actually held in my hands these two creatures that seemed to be so alive caused a sensation of wonder that I have never forgotten. When I was in Paris in the sixties, I met Bergen's movie star daughter, Candice, when she came over to make a film in the French language, *Vivre pour vivre* (*Live for Life* in the U.S.). However, I just couldn't bring myself to tell her I had met her father and held her "brothers," by then ensconced in America's Smithsonian Museum in Washington, D.C. People in the publicity field must never let the mask slip and allow the "talent" to know, even for a moment, that you might in some way show that you are in awe of anything or anyone being associated with them. It is no more than part of the job and woe be he or she who forgets it.

Another major Hollywood involvement during those years in the late forties was when the famous 20th Century Fox production head Darryl F. Zanuck sent a team of his top publicity and advertising people to the Bay Area to start preparations for the first release of *Forever Amber*, starring Linda Darnell. This had been a wildly successful best-selling book and was already the most hyped movie of that time. However, now that it was about to be released, there was a great deal of conjecture among the Fox hierarchy about whether it was going to be successful because it was a "costume drama." I remember when Zanuck ordered all his pub-ad types together to discuss how the picture should best be sold as the whole campaign approach was suddenly being questioned. I was permitted to be present and sit quietly in a corner. Someone said, "Well, in the advertising let us feature the actors' faces only and not show the costumes." I personally thought this was a bit crazy, considering that, up until that point, the picture had been sold as the biggest bodice-ripper ever made, and millions had obviously read the book and were very well aware of the subject matter. How such a suggestion could even be considered was beyond me, but nevertheless, this was what was said. It was my first exposure to what could happen to sane and intelligent people when "panic" set in. A wrong suggestion at this level could put one's livelihood in big jeopardy. As the most junior person in the room, I certainly wasn't called upon to speak (thank God!) but I did feel whatever I might have said could not have been more stupid than some of the suggestions made that day. While an eventual success of sorts, the film of *Forever Amber* was never as big as the book.

Another magic memory was a two day visit of the most famous star in the world at the time, John Wayne. He came up to promote the release of his film *The Angel and the Badman*. He was accompanied by his manager and his personal publicist. This was to be another good lesson for me as it was the first time I had to coordinate what was being done with someone else whose only interest was to promote and keep happy an individual star—and was not present just to promote the film. I was somewhat in awe of being in the presence of the box-office king of the movies. However, with all respect to Wayne, after two days I came to the conclusion that he was just another major actor with whom I had to work and, most importantly, not upset in the process.

My San Francisco Interlude was an ongoing and never-ending education.

26

Upperclassman Years

Having come to the conclusion that my future was not to be with her husband selling check-writers, Bunny Maysuch asked if I would be agreeable to having her son, by now one of the world's major film stars at 20th Century–Fox, speak about me to the head of the studio's publicity department, the larger than life Harry Brand. I learned later why Brand had not been up to San Francisco for the *Forever Amber* meetings. He was clever enough to delegate his number two, as there were other "very important" matters needing his singular attention at the New York office, and company president Spyros Skouras insisted he be there. That Zanuck accepted his absence in San Francisco was always a mystery to me, even though he was second to Skouras in the pecking order. Obviously, Harry knew where the "bodies were buried," and by delegating, he was careful to avoid blame if the picture flopped! He had obviously trumped the card of his company "vice president/head of production" with the one that read "president!" One didn't survive at the top in Hollywood without a touch of Machiavelli, and Harry Brand was a master. Another lesson learned!

Though I felt that being considered for a job as the "friend" of a star was not the way to get into a studio, I agreed to go down to LA and, taking a couple of days off, I stayed with Greg and his then wife Greta. I duly met with Brand, and within a few minutes I knew this idea of Bunny's was not going to work out. I sat there in his big office while he took a call, loudly announced by his secretary to be from Walter Winchell, the famed New York columnist. At the end of the call (which I doubt was real to this day) Brand said, "Sorry, there are no openings available at this time, maybe later." He wished me well and I was ushered out the door. I was in his office for some ten minutes and for about seven he was on the phone. He knew he would have no problem with Peck, as I wasn't a relative or really close friend. We met at a couple of industry functions sometime later when I was an established studio publicity man, but I never alluded to my once asking him for a job and that I might have been at Fox instead of Paramount. When I finally worked at Fox as an associate in production with the Arthur Jacobs Company (*Planet of the Apes*, etc.), Brand was gone, though I did enjoy a certain frisson the first time I was in a meeting in Harry's old office.

Back in San Francisco, I soon had another opportunity offered when the major cinema/distribution company Paramount Pictures Theaters Corporation offered me a job in their Northern California publicity department.

It was the start of many moves in and out of various divisions of Paramount for me spanning some twenty years.

A first for me happened around this time when Bing Crosby came up for a location shoot of a few scenes at the Tanforan Racetrack in nearby San Bruno for *Riding High*. Paramount's field man for Northern California, who coordinated all the exploitation (see the aside at the end of this chapter) of the company's films in that area, arranged for me to visit the set. Though it was quite something to meet Bing (little did I know how friendly we were to become), it was getting to say "Hello" to one of the greatest names in the history of motion picture comedy that really meant something to me. I am referring to the great Oliver Hardy, whom Bing had arranged to have a small role in the film. He was in but one scene and played a horse race enthusiast overwhelmed with indecision as he plied his way through newspapers and betting pamphlets while trying to decide on which horse was to be the winner. I count myself very lucky to have it arranged to have been there, stand off camera, and watch Hardy "act." It was a true thrill, one of my top moments on a film set anywhere at any time. That first experience is also memorable because it was to be Hardy's final time ever on screen.

With Bing Crosby (right) at Paramount, 1950s (Paramount).

Over many months I worked on quite a few movies that Paramount screened or premiered in the Bay Area. Two of their big money making B-film producers came up on two or three occasions. They were Bill Pine and Bill Thomas (known as the Dollar Bills). Their top actors were no longer major names but were still box office draws in a well-made production with a popular theme—people like Ronald Reagan, John Payne, and Rhonda Fleming. There was a well-known joke at the time about Payne; except for a "P" instead of a "W," he would be the Number One movie star in the nation.

I quickly developed a good relationship with the two Bills and it was directly through this association that I came to the attention of Norman Siegel, the director of the Publicity Department at Paramount (Pine's old job). One day I received a call from him regarding the planned arrival of the great star from the silent days, Gloria Swanson, for a publicity tour that was starting in San Francisco for the release of *Sunset Boulevard*. He wanted to be certain that when she was there she was handled with care, diligence, and understanding. I wondered at the time why no one from the studio's publicity department was along, even though the Northern California field man was much in evidence.

I did find out why many months later—it was a test of my ability. I guess I was successful, as I got another unsolicited signed photo when Swanson left for the next city. She had been very nice, but somewhat distant. At least I got to know what a loyal courtier at Buckingham Palace must feel like working in close proximity to Her Majesty the Queen. However, I will never forget one "non-royal" meeting in her suite toward the end of her visit when she talked with me while standing on her head with her feet propped up against the wall. This was her yoga position to re-energize her 50-something-year-old body. She was one of the most professional actors I ever met and would do almost anything required if she felt it was good for the selling of her or her film.

It was not too long after when I received another call from Siegel asking if I could come down and meet about a possible position in his department. *Could I ??!!* I quickly flew south and he duly offered me a position as a junior publicist at the princely sum (to me) of $125 a week. I jumped at the chance and so began a six-year period that really was one of the great times of my life, both professionally and socially.

Before closing the chapter on San Francisco, I should mention that on very few occasions when multiple films were opening, it was a necessity for me to write a couple of film reviews for a few of the foreign language films that opened from time-to-time in this most cosmopolitan American city. I was paid (not much). The paper was the famous *Chronicle*, and though my name was never given a byline, I was fortunate to learn some of the mentality of journalists from the inside. People like the paper's young city editor, Pierre Salinger—later to be famous as press secretary to President Kennedy. That background didn't hurt years later when he was European correspondent for ABC, one of the Big Three of TV news, and I was responsible for coverage for James Bond.

A woman I was dating at this time was a dear friend of a young lady who was a regular of the San Francisco nightclub life. Through this connection I became friends with the famous singer Mel Tormé. Our mutual interest in World War I aviation history led to a quick friendship. His tales of his early days as a contract player at MGM mesmerized me and added to my belief that life in Hollywood certainly had its attractions. He told me a story of the first meeting between the newly signed starlet Ava Gardner and the uptight young Englishman, Peter Lawford. Lawford was coming on to Gardner in a very English upper-class twit manner, and she shut him up, according to Tormé, by suddenly asking, "Do you eat pussy?" This had me laughing for

A one-off drawing of the author by former *Daily Express* cartoonist Charles Griffin (author's collection).

days. The earthy country girl from North Carolina certainly had a way with words! Many years later, I was to learn this first hand in Madrid (to be discussed in a later chapter).

*   *   *

I should point out that in his monumental work, *The International Film Encyclopedia*, author Ephraim Katz describes an important difference in the promotion of feature films:

> Exploitation: The combined use of advertising, public relations and other forms of promotion and sales techniques for the purpose of realizing the profit potential of a film.

> Publicist: A person in the film industry engaged in the promotion and publicity aspects of a motion picture studio, i.e., preparing press releases, planting items in newspapers, tipping off columnists, securing publicity skills, arranging press conferences and special premieres, and generally seeking the greatest exposure for his company's films and stars.

The chief publicist of a studio is known as "publicity director." Today, however, anything relating to all areas of promotion later now comes under the mantle of "marketing."

The Last
of the Golden Years

Paramount—My Early Days

In the spring of 1950 I reported for work at Paramount Studios, one of three actually situated within the borders of the town of Hollywood itself. Of the three, two were majors: Columbia and Paramount. The other, RKO, was considered a mini-major, much to the chagrin of famous owners over time like Joseph Kennedy and Howard Hughes. The RKO lot shared a common wall with Paramount, so the two were literally cheek-to-jowl. One of the great vistas in the Hollywood of the fifties was of the two giant water towers (one with the Paramount logo emblazoned on its side, and the other with RKO Radio) standing within a couple of hundred yards of each other.

Paramount was laid out in a rectangular shape facing a short street of a few blocks grandiosely named Marathon Avenue. Near the center was the famous iron grilled gate. The publicity department was at one far end and at the other was the Cecil B. DeMille building with its own gate. Taking up most of the frontage in between was the executive block with the main walk-in entrance in the center. Upon entering there was a large square around which were buildings that housed departments for art, costumes, music, and more. The street to the left was "Dressing Room Row" in the heart of the studio, where I was to spend many hours of my life for six years. We in publicity called this "Star Alley." The overall spacious quarters of Hope and Crosby reflected their status as the studio's top money-makers at the time.

The executive offices were in the two-story main block along with legal and casting and such. The offices of producers and directors were also principally located in this building. The various sound stages took up some two-thirds of the "plant." The back lot at the rear reached the rear wall with the giant Hollywood Cemetery on the other side.

Scattered hither and yon were the sound, camera, and construction departments that all contributed to the making of a finished motion picture. A film studio was a self-contained factory with the end product a few reels

In my first office at Paramount. Note the sample Oscars on my desk (Paramount Pictures)!

of 35mm film to be projected in cinemas around the world as a couple of hours of entertainment and escape for literally millions of the human race. This giant audience felt they "knew" the glamorous figures upon the screen and reveled in the stories of their private lives. The fairy-tales from La La Land (that state-of-mind place called Hollywood) was the stuff of dreams, a non-health-threatening opiate for the common man.

To those working behind the walls of the studios, it was what we did. It was like being backstage watching a magic act. You saw how the illusion was done and enjoyed its creation, but you also were aware it was all just part of a business called entertainment.

Everything that happened later in my career that was positive had its genesis in those six years during the 1950s, a period now known as the Last of the Golden Age of Hollywood. I feel very fortunate to have been there for that endgame and to have been in a position to interact on a daily basis with so very many of Hollywood's most famous creative people of the day.

Every studio had its contracted "house" actors, producers, directors, composers, and such, and Paramount's talent was as good as it got in the early to mid-fifties. The actors under studio contract or who were signed by one of the major producers and/or directors based there were:

Gene Barry	Mona Freeman	Grace Kelly	Shirley MacLaine
William Bendix	Audrey Hepburn	Oreste Kirkop	Dean Martin
Yul Brynner	Charlton Heston	Alan Ladd	Ray Milland
Rosemary Clooney	William Holden	Dorothy Lamour	Anthony Perkins
Wendell Corey	Bob Hope	Burt Lancaster	Elvis Presley
Bing Crosby	Betty Hutton	Jerry Lewis	Lizabeth Scott
Pat Crowley	Carolyn Jones	Sophia Loren	Jan Sterling
Kirk Douglas	Danny Kaye	John Lund	Henry Wilcoxon
Rhonda Fleming			

Actors who came to Paramount to make one or more films during those years included:

Eddie Albert	Yvonne de Carlo	Janet Leigh	Thelma Ritter
June Allyson	Marlene Dietrich	Vivien Leigh	Edward G. Robinson
Louis Armstrong	Vera Ellen	Sophia Loren	Ginger Rogers
Jean Arthur	Peter Finch	Anna Magnani	Mickey Rooney
Fred Astaire	Joan Fontaine	Karl Malden	Jane Russell
Anne Baxter	Clark Gable	Fredric March	Rosalind Russell
Humphrey Bogart	Mitzi Gaynor	Patricia Medina	Frank Sinatra
Shirley Booth	Gloria Grahame	Terry Moore	James Stewart
Marlon Brando	Cary Grant	Patricia Neal	Elizabeth Taylor
James Cagney	Lee Grant	Lloyd Nolan	Gene Tierney
George Chakiris	Van Heflin	Laurence Olivier	Spencer Tracy
Montgomery Clift	Katharine Hepburn	Jack Palance	Peter Ustinov
Nat (King) Cole	Glynis Johns	Cecil Parker	Robert Wagner
Joan Crawford	Jennifer Jones	Eleanor Parker	Robert Walker
Tony Curtis	Deborah Kerr	George Peppard	Cornel Wilde
Doris Day	Fernando Lamas	Anthony Perkins	Shelley Winters

Producers, directors, and/or writers included, among others:

Charles Brackett	Alfred Hitchcock	William Perlberg	William Thomas
Frederick Brisson	Mitchell Leisen	William Pine	Hal Wallis
Cecil B. DeMille	George Marshall	George Seaton	Billy Wilder
John Farrow	Leo McCarey	George Stevens	William Wyler

Major composers included:

Irving Berlin	Ray Evans	Johnny Mercer	James Van Heusen
Sammy Cahn	Burton Lane	Alex North	Franz Waxman
Hoagy Carmichael	Jay Livingstone		

When I joined the publicity department I became the most junior member of a group of some thirty very professional men and women whose main priority was selling the product and the very special people who made that product. Massaging egos and keeping certain "news" out of the public eye was a part of the job, too, and not to be underestimated in importance.

The casting director was always adding new young hopefuls to our contract list and I quickly found out that the guys and gals who made up the department membership would have a draw after each new signing as to how long it would take that particular newcomer to say or do something that meant we in publicity were no longer a best and much needed friend, but rather more of a lesser being who is around to be of service to the demands of a newly arrived STAR!

The all-time record between signing a contract and showing signs of being holier than thou was the young Texan Kathryn Grandstaff—soon to be named Kathryn Grant. She also didn't need too long to grab the brass ring by getting a gold one from Bing Crosby. After wife Dixie's death, we had all been pulling for Mona Freeman, a real sweetheart, but that was really wishful thinking. I guess we had read too many scripts with a happy ending!

Whose life was it anyway?

My first assignment was as a "planter." Cecil "Teet" Carle, the assistant publicity director, and James "Andy" Hervey, the head planter, were ex-MGM publicists from the pre-war era, so they were among the very best from whom one could hope to "learn the ropes." The head planter handled the top of the journalistic tree: giants like Louella Parsons and Hedda Hopper in LA and Walter Winchell in New York. As one of the assistants, I was to be responsible for feeding news and information, gossip and tidbits ("planting") to people like Sheila Graham, who came to Hollywood from England after the war and became somewhat famous in her own right as the live-in lover of the famed novelist F. Scott Fitzgerald. By my time she was third in importance of the many show-business columnists. Louella and Hedda each wielded enough power to make or break careers, and Sheila was determined to become a member of this unholy alliance.

Another journalist to whom I was assigned was Erskine Johnson, a marvelous wire-service veteran and a very nice guy in the bargain. Sidney Skolsky was also great to work with. I handled a whole group of columnists who were on various important papers around the country. The best known of these were Irv Kupcinet, Herb Caen, and Earl Wilson. Giving items to Caen was a continuation of my contact with him from San Francisco. If there was any Northern California angle, I "fed" it to Herb and it appeared like clockwork. The two Hollywood trade papers and their respective columnists also became my assignment when Andy was otherwise engaged. Out of those earliest days I forged a close association and friendship with the legendary Army Archerd of *Daily Variety*, who at that time was the "legman" for the veteran Harrison Carroll nearing the end of his career. Servicing the giant wire-service entities, Associated Press and United Press, also became my remit, and stalwarts like Bob Thomas, Jim Bacon, Aline Mosby, and Vernon Scott were my confidants in all things Hollywood with the obvious emphasis on whatever might be in the best interest of Paramount's product and players.

This was my principal function for quite some time but my secondary duty must be mentioned. In the days long before studio tours became a way-of-Hollywood-life, visitors who were deemed of sufficient importance had to be personally shown what a studio looked like and to be given a small taste of its day-to-day life. Separate to watching a scene being filmed on one of the sound stages, everyone always enjoyed walking along the different streets representing the Wild West, New York, or Paris on the large back lot. It was left to the junior members of the publicity department to guide these VIPs so, as the new boy, it mostly fell to me. I very soon got to know every nook and cranny of Paramount as well as getting to meet many people I otherwise might not have encountered in my normal duties. For example, most of the studio cops became friends on a first name basis, and often this was to prove a very special help to me over the years. It was all part of my learning curve, and while I certainly enjoyed it at first, being a tour guide became a little tedious.

Eventually, by sheer dint of time and seniority, this duty ended. However, if a really important member of the world press came visiting (usually with family on tow), I would often be asked to accompany them. Anyway, I enjoyed getting to know the studio and soon came to be known to one and all within its walls.

*   *   *

My re-encounter with Bob Hope is a good place to begin my Hollywood years. I went over and introduced myself to his brother Jack, who ran Bob Hope Enterprises from Bob's double-sized dressing room. I asked Jack to tell Bob of my brief time as his army liaison and that I just wished to reintroduce myself and pay my respects. Obviously, Hope was a man who met thousands of people and I did try my best to tell Jack to let him know that I wasn't look-ing for anything, I just wanted him to know that I was there. I soon got a call back from Jack to say that Bob wanted to see me. He was a bit guarded in demeanor when we met, and of course said he remembered me (after all he *was* an accomplished actor separate to being one of the most famous come-dians in the world).

I explained that I was now working at the studio and he said that, to his knowledge, I was the only member of the military assigned to accompany one of his countless shows throughout the war who was now working at Para-mount. This seemed to amuse him. I really think this started what became a close working relationship between us.

The assistant publicity director, a very laid-back veteran of the pre-war MGM Studio, which was the ultimate at the time, took me around the lot to

The author (third from left) with publicist Art Sarno (fourth from left) in a light moment between takes with Bob Hope (center) and columnist Harrison Carroll (far right) on the Paramount lot. Lou Schurr, Hope's longtime agent, looks on (Paramount).

The author (right) meeting Alfred Hitchcock again, Paris, 1950s. The man at left is unidentified (Paramount France).

introduce me to many of those with whom I would soon be interacting. I particularly remember meeting Alfred Hitchcock and, a few years later, his new young actress on the set of his comedy/mystery, *The Trouble with Harry*. The soon to be star in her first film was Shirley MacLaine. I had never heard of the leading man, a very young John Forsythe. *Dynasty* and TV superstardom were years away.

I also recall Bob Hope saying when we met him in the street near his dressing room—"Oh, I've known Jerry from the army in Europe." I'll never forget the reaction I got from my new boss. I tried to look innocent by quickly explaining that I didn't know we were even meeting Hope on that introductory walk-about.

Of the actors there during my early months, one who impressed me very much was John Lund, a genuinely nice man who would have been a success in any field. He never really became a big star, but he had a big human spirit and a selfless quality that was unique. It was good for me to know early on that most "working actors" were not egomaniacs and that there were some genuinely nice people who treated acting as a profession and not an exercise in being "rich and famous." There were too many who expected to be treated as demi-gods and they considered lesser mortals such as we in publicity, at best, as a necessary evil. Great to be around if needed, but a bit of a bother the majority of the time. I quickly learned to also be very guarded in action, work, and demeanor when dealing with the "talent." Like a lion tamer, exciting to work with the "big cats," but don't turn your back or you just might get bitten!

My duties meant I had to spend a lot of time on the different sets of films in production even those "closed sets" that were secret except to an approved studio functionary. One of the most "open" of sets was a romantic-comedy being filmed there entitled *The Mating Season*, starring Lund and one of the most beautiful actresses (at least in my opinion) of all time, Gene Tierney. I should mention that back when I was in Europe in the army there were two or three films that were shown time and again to the troops whenever they were in a reserve position and able to look at a 16mm print projected onto a sheet hung up against a wall in a darkened hall. One of those was Crosby in *Going My Way* and another was the 20th Century–Fox film *Laura*, which made a star of Tierney. About every GI fell in love with her and thought she was a most exquisite creature, certainly not the proverbial girl next door nor the Betty Grable type of glamorous pin-up. Anyway, it was quite something for me to now be "working" with her and to find that she was a very sweet and lovely individual. She was married to the mercurial French American dress designer Oleg Cassini. Not known at that time, they were in what were to be the last months of their tumultuous marriage.

One day I had to go see Tierney in her on-set portable dressing room about some interview. Suddenly, Cassini came barging in. He was very mad and started to call her (in French) every name in the book. Of course, neither of them was aware that I understood quite a bit of the language and they both obviously assumed that they could say whatever they wanted in my presence, no matter how personal. Anyway, after he really berated her for three or four minutes and she was close to tears, it all became just too uncomfortable and I decided that I wasn't going to let this pass. So, during a brief lull in his diatribe, I said to Gene—in French—"Excuse me, I think it is time for me to go." Of course, they were both somewhat thunderstruck that I had not spoken English and their verbal fighting came to a thundering halt as I walked out. Later in the day when I was back on the set, she called me over and apologized for their conversation in my presence and said that she thought I handled a bad situation with tact and finesse. With a kind of a twinkle in her eye, she leaned forward and gave me a very sweet little kiss of thanks, as it had been a put-down of Cassini in her mind.

Anyway, I really thought she was a lovely person and was very pleased at the close-of-picture party when she handed me an envelope containing a signed picture addressed "To Jerry from Gene, with Love." I have always treasured the photo and the reason for having it. Of course, it is now well-known that their life together was one of much unhappiness as a result of the awful tragedy surrounding her daughter's birth. There was a certain quiet sadness to Gene. She never verbalized or showed it openly. After all, she *was* an actress. The story was that a newly pregnant Tierney was one of the stars present at the Hollywood Canteen one evening during World War II when servicemen were entertained by the famous. Years later, at some function, a woman approached Gene, excitedly telling her that she was her favorite star and, though feeling sick, the woman, then a member of the Women's Army Corps, got out of bed to meet Tierney. It had been publicized that she would be one of the stars present that night. The woman told Tierney she went into the hospital within days with chicken pox, but she got to meet the actress. It was a horror of Shakespearean proportions, for Tierney's only child was born severely disabled as a result of the mother having contracted rubella during pregnancy.

It is of interest that in the screenplay of Agatha Christie's *The Mirror Crack'd* (starring Elizabeth Taylor and Rock Hudson), this real-life happening of Tierney's was used as the major plot point in the dénouement of the mystery.

* * *

In my "Book of Unusual Memories," going to New York as the chaperon/guide/adviser for the early-fifties newly-formed edition of Paramount's

40

Golden Circle (a select group of the studio's young, bright, and beautiful contract players) was a unique experience, and it gave a studio-based publicist a rare chance to interact directly with some of the company's New York home office publicity people. "Never the twain shall meet" seemed to be the rule for some reason I've never fathomed.

Of the pre-war members of the Golden Circle, I believe only Susan Hayward went on to become a star. Of my edition, Mary Murphy (Marlon Brando's co-star in *The Wild One*) was the only contemporary success. The other to make it was Marion Ross, who gained fame as the mother of Richie in the long-running wildly successful family comedy TV show *Happy Days*. An interesting commentary on perception. Of the half dozen or so of the starlets, Marion was the least likely to win a Miss America beauty pageant, as she was neither wildly buxom nor beautiful. However, she was one of those rare women who became prettier the longer you were around her. It didn't hurt that that she was also a very talented actress, which directly reflected on her long and successful career.

None of the males in the group achieved much except for a very handsome young Frenchman, Jacques Bergerac. His main claim to fame was to become Ginger Rogers' husband. She was on the lot around that time starring in one of her last films, *Forever Female*. Her co-star was Pat Crowley, a bright and breezy young actress, already too established at the studio to be in the Golden Circle when we went to New York. I really thought Pat might be one of the few to make the higher echelon of stardom, and Paramount put a lot of time and effort into her career, but the "fickle finger of fate" was to decide otherwise; close, but no prize. The Hollywood treadmill of success was not a kind and caring one. However, that aside, it was interesting to observe two actresses, one at the end of a world-famous career and the other at "breakthrough" time appearing together. A bit of *All About Eve* in real life—without the bitchiness and rancor.

At the close-of-picture party, I got up my courage and asked Ginger for a dance as our respective tables were side-by-side, and it seemed to be appropriate to take advantage of a once-in-a-lifetime opportunity. She graciously accepted and gave me three minutes of wonder. As for Miss Crowley, she became a major star of TV. Better small screen than no screen at all.

*   *   *

A happening that helped my career as a planter came about quite accidentally. The Hollywood make-up artists had joined together to celebrate their craft by having an annual dinner-dance featuring the presence of all the young actresses under contract at the various studios. One such gathering took place in September of 1955 at the Hollywood Palladium. Each studio took a few tables and invited various press to be there as their guests and to sit with the "future stars." Paramount's main invitee was the redoubtable Hedda Hopper.

As I was pulling up to the front of the Palladium, a flash announcement came over my car radio that Associated Press had just reported that movie star James Dean had been killed in an automobile accident up near San Francisco. In those days, long before the personal mobile phone, there was no way word would have got to the press already assembled. I ran inside and knowing exactly where Paramount's tables were, rushed up to Hedda and told her the news. As she shot out of her chair to a phone, actress Pier Angeli (with MGM) was temporarily visiting the Paramount table where her sister Marisa Pavan was sitting. Angeli, the girlfriend of Dean at the time, overheard my telling Hedda of the tragedy. She went into a kind of shock and became quite agitated. Hedda had a scoop based on this in-person reaction. She later told Norman Siegel, our head of publicity and the man responsible for my employment, that in the future she wanted me to handle her when her regular Paramount planter was not available. Of course, this pleased Norman and didn't hurt me one little bit.

Onward and upward!!

Paramount—The Middle Years

Many columnists from near and far would come to LA to visit the studios and I would get to know them by being their contact and/or guide when they came to our lot. I particularly remember Earl Wilson from New York and Irv Kupcinet from Chicago as being everything one imagined a top-flight newspaper man to be. Kupcinet had a lovely daughter who was an aspiring actress. She did make it to Hollywood, but early in her career she was tragically murdered. Naturally her death almost destroyed Irv and his wife, and all of us who knew them felt it was a tragedy doubled since the case was never solved. It seemed there was never sufficient proof to pin the murder on the individual many considered the most likely suspect.

My association with both Hope and Crosby became very close over the years and I was quite pleased to have been personally asked by Bing to be in attendance to handle the press at the funeral of his first wife, Dixie. There was one awkward moment when a very experienced photographer from one of the main Los Angeles papers got so carried away that he forgot the sad circumstance of why we were all there and said, to the horror of those within earshot, "One more by the casket, Bing." With a quick expression of "Sorry" from me, I moved all the photographers away, calming down what was embarrassing for all. The life of a Hollywood publicist could be quite hairy at times, no doubt about it!

We had two major romantic action stars under contract—William Holden and Alan Ladd. Both were very aware of the value of promoting their films, but, like all actors, were always mindful of image and self. I liked them both but became closer to Bill over the years. While Alan was not an easy man to get close to, he was basically a nice guy. His agent/wife Sue Carol had a lot to do with his reserve in my opinion. I would get to know Alan Junior in London a couple of decades later when "Laddie" was a successful producer, a very nice person, and a very good reflection of his father.

The author (second from left) on the tarmac in Berlin with Boris Jankovich, Paramount's distribution chief for Germany (third from left), star William Holden and an unidentified woman as an airline employee leads the way, early 1960s.

One of my most vivid recollections of those years involved Holden. It was the night of the 1953 Academy Awards at the Pantages Theater on Hollywood Boulevard (held in early 1954). Whenever a major personality from the studio was nominated for one of the big awards, a publicist was assigned to be there to help handle matters as needed. Bill was my responsibility that night and when he won Best Actor for *Stalag 17*. There was joy in the world, *until* Bill and his wife, Brenda Marshall, got in the limo (along with me in attendance) to drive to the party to celebrate the evening and his win. There we were, Bill and Brenda in the back seat and me in the jump seat facing him. As we were pulling away Ardis (her real name) leaned forward, looked at Bill, who was proudly holding the statue, and bitterly said, "You didn't deserve that." I must note here that she never seemed to forgive Bill for her having given up an acting career at Warner Bros. to marry and raise a family (two great sons). Holden's fingers turned white with rage as his fist tightened around his Oscar. I thought he was going to swing it at her—and possibly hit me first since I was sitting knee to knee opposite. Fortunately, his anger held and the moment passed. Later on that night, Bill more than made up for the earlier hours of abstention. He certainly had a lot of reasons to get loaded and who could blame him? I could never watch Bill on the screen again without that Oscar evening in the back of my mind. To me, a great actor and a great guy. The last time I was ever drunk "out of my skull" was thanks to Bill. I woke up on his living-room chintz-covered sofa at his house in San Fernando Valley.

A signed photograph from Cecil B. DeMille (author's collection).

Another Academy Award night to remember was when I left the theater to walk to the waiting limo while carrying

Cecil B. DeMille's Irving Thalberg Award in one hand and the Oscar (for Best Picture *The Greatest Show on Earth*) in my other. As I handed them over to C. B., before his car pulled away, little did I know that we would meet one day some five years later in a suite at the Grand Hotel in Rome, Italy, before going to the Vatican for his audience with the Pope! More on that later.

The show business "fan" in me (buried deep in my psyche) came slightly to the fore at one of those magic Academy backstage moments when I had to lead Maurice Chevalier to his position in the wings before he went on stage to receive an honorary Oscar. I think it was one of the ultimate moments of rehabilitation for him from the misplaced charges of collaboration during the World War II occupation of France. When Nazi Germany overran France in 1940, Chevalier was probably the most famous Frenchman in the world. Thousands of French soldiers were in POW camps and Chevalier accepted the offer by the German victors to entertain them in captivity. After the liberation, many accused Chevalier of aiding the enemy. By his actions, whatever the motivation, he soon regained his stardom at home and abroad. At any rate, I was very pleased to briefly be able to speak to him in French and wish him "good luck" before he went on stage. He seemed pleased to hear his own language spoken (even my bad version of it) at that nervous moment. Even a show-business giant gets the few odd tremors of nervousness from time to time. They're all human, though there are times that many do not seem to know that obvious fact!

One day I received a call in my office from the cop at the main gate. Someone had just phoned him to say he was accidentally locked in at a certain sound stage and was most unhappy. The cop was concerned that it might be a good idea if a studio public relations type was there when the door was unlocked. I met our policeman and he opened the door, whereby who was to step out but a somewhat agitated Cary Grant with his agent in tow. Not bothering to ask how they came to be locked in an empty stage in the late afternoon, I asked, "Cary, why didn't you tell the gate who you were?" He replied that he did, but the cop wouldn't believe it was actually him calling. I then said, "Maybe he didn't recognize your voice." Even though it was well known that his was probably the most imitated and famous voice of all the stars in the world, Mister Grant (he of no sense of humor) was not amused. Later on, the fact that his co-star and "good friend" Sophia Loren seemed to like me around did not change his manner. To me he was one cold fish.

The concept of one being overly serious about one's work is not necessarily a bad thing, but it can't be mentioned without thinking of a very intense

The author (in sunglasses) checks out the cameraman while escorting Sophia Loren through the streets of Vienna, 1950s.

young actor of the time named Charlton Heston, who had signed a contract only a few months before I joined the Publicity Department. A few of us there privately nicknamed him "Chuckles" for obvious reasons. I got to become fairly good friends with him over the many years that followed in Hollywood and around the world. "Chuck" (his name to one and all) was as nice down deep as he was serious on the surface. For me, a great actor and a great American.

When we were together in Cairo and London on *Khartoum*, I heard Laurence Olivier say that he thought Heston's English accent was the best of any American actor. I admired "Chuck" for many reasons. A real man in the best sense. Far too many of those I knew in those years have passed away in the last couple of decades, but when Heston died, I felt a sadness at the loss of someone for whom I held great admiration.

I first met Laurence/Larry/Sir/Lord Olivier when he came to Paramount to star opposite Jennifer Jones in the film of Theodore Dreiser's classic novel,

Sister Carrie. He was always someone special to us at the studio. Of all the foreign actors and actresses who worked there during those years, Larry had that touch of class and breeding which always kept us "colonials" a bit wrong-footed and slightly in awe when dealing with him. However, events were to transpire which were to pay off for me a few years later in London when trust became the most important factor in our workplace. Fate was yet again knocking at my door. This all came about a year or two later when Mrs. Olivier, better known to the movie-going world as Vivien Leigh, came to Paramount to star in a major film, *Elephant Walk.* Her co-stars were long-time Hollywood leading man Dana Andrews, and also Peter Finch, the very ballsy Australian star of the wonderful *A Town Like Alice.* I have known many actors who were successful with the ladies—men who were handsome and charismatic, much less being a famous movie-star, but never have I encountered anyone quite his equal. If it wore a skirt and breathed, he had it. No one in my six years there cut a swath through the female employees at the studio like Peter Finch. Maybe it was the Christian name that they had in common, but Peter O'Toole came the closest to matching his libido, at least in my observation. May I note that Bill Holden was no slouch either in this regard.

Elephant Walk started on location in Ceylon (now Sri Lanka) and word soon filtered back to the studio of problems with Leigh. When the company returned, it became apparent that Vivien was at the point of total exhaustion. The problem was primarily due to Finch. That they had a location affair (big deal) while on the island was not surprising, but it was taken a little too seriously by Leigh, with disastrous results. Actually, she was mentally and physically wasted, a very high-strung and fragile personality at the best of times. She was unable to handle the inevitability of age and the fading of her incredible beauty. The location affair with Finch would have been short-lived anyway, but Vivien became convinced it was due to her appearance. The rumor was that she did everything possible to remain awake because she felt that every time she slept she would awaken looking older. It is easy to understand her disintegration but more difficult to comprehend the dark side of someone once called the world's most beautiful woman. Her condition quickly worsened and filming came to a complete halt. Leigh was fired by Paramount. It was obvious that the production had to continue with another leading lady.

Many names were considered and finally, at quite some cost, Elizabeth Taylor came over from MGM to take Leigh's place. There is one brief long shot from the Ceylon location in the final cut where the actress is Leigh, and that's it.

Olivier came out to LA and, with the help of his good friend Danny Kaye, arrangements were made for her to be flown home. The first step was from the rented Beverly Hills residence to the airport in Burbank for her to be placed on board an ambulance plane for a first stage flight to New York. Kaye particularly asked the studio that I be at the airport to be of assistance if needed. All went well and, with little fuss or bother, the middle of the night flight took off, leaving me a lonely figure to make my way to my home in Beverly Glen.

Vivien did recover back in England and enjoyed much more acclaim and success.

* * *

The author (left) dining with Pat Crowley (second from left), Buddy Ebsen (third from left), and Gene Barry (right), others unidentified, on a studio publicity trip for *Red Garters*, Dallas, 1954 (Paramount).

Whenever there was a tour arranged to promote one of our films, it seemed that Texas was quite often the venue and it was usually me who Norman Siegel decided would accompany the personalities. Sometimes, if it was a sizable group, a publicist would also be assigned from the New York office. This was a recipe for a counterproductive situation, as it was enough worrying about the actors and their egos without two publicists concerned with where the credit went for a successful and productive tour. But that was the decision of those in charge, and in spite of the odd bruising of sensitivities, we always seemed to muddle through.

One of the more interesting tours was for a highly stylized and innovative western titled *Red Garters*. Pat Crowley, singer Guy Mitchell, as well as Gene Barry and Buddy Ebsen (future major TV stars), were to spend a couple of weeks in Dallas, Houston, and San Antonio. It made for a pleasant change from the usual studio routine. Unfortunately, Rosemary Clooney wasn't free at the time.

It was also educational to find that show business journalists were more difficult when on their own turf than when visiting Hollywood. It was yet another lesson in the handling of media types whose output in newspapers, magazines, and TV/radio contributed to a successful campaign. The bottom line was that we in publicity needed the fourth estate as much as they needed us and more often than not, it seemed to work out to the satisfaction (and benefit) of all concerned.

*   *   *

For a studio publicist, the biggest challenge was to be given the job in the first place. An analogy would be that of a baseball player getting to the Big Leagues. Being chosen was the difficult part, staying was another country. However, once in one had to continually cement his or her position by becoming known, needed, and indispensable to the talent and, more importantly, those in charge.

I cultivated heavyweights like costume designer Edith Head and composer Johnny Mercer, along with many of the lawyers whose decisions were so important in every day studio life. The head of the studio was Y. Frank Freeman, famous as one of the top brains from the exhibition side of the industry. He was a courtly Georgia gentleman (the complete antithesis of the public persona of a Hollywood mogul) and was particularly friendly (my Southern connections didn't hurt!). It was a pleasure to be on the outer fringes of the innermost circle and become accepted as an insider. "Speak when spoken to and offer a constructive suggestion or opinion only when directly asked" was the order of the day whenever circumstances put me in the proximity of this center of power at Paramount.

The biggest no-no for all studio personnel was to openly second guess any decision of the head of production. Once a film was announced as going into production, it was professional suicide to speak ill of it. We in the Publicity Department would certainly talk among ourselves as to the decisions made and the problems that would be faced trying to sell some of the turkeys that would appear from time to time on the production treadmill, but, God forbid, that such words of doubt or derision ever reached the ears of the company's senior power brokers. Wherever in the world motion pictures were made or released, I found this mantra to hold true, and it was followed as gospel by all those in the various ranks below the decision makers.

* * *

For about six months I was assigned to assist in the department that handled the products (mainly spirits and cigarettes) that were advertised in print media and on radio. This paid advertising would feature a glamorous head shot of the actors concerned endorsing the product and saluting the taste, pleasure, and quality (whatever) involved. All with a big credit for the Paramount film in release. Product placement had not yet become a factor in the marketing of films, but the straightforward star endorsement in the fifties certainly was the forerunner of that promotional tool that was a couple of decades away from becoming an industrywide practice. I was given a key to the large closet crammed with bottles, cartons, and a cornucopia of clothing, toys, and electrical products. Eventually I was put in charge of this arm of the department and became amazed at the reaction of some of the stars who, through making very big bucks, would almost grovel in pursuit of "freebies." I particularly remember one long-time Paramount romantic lead, Ray Milland, who used to greet me with effusive delight whenever I showed up at his dressing-room with a "delivery."

One of the biggest promotions I personally set up was for Bob Hope's film *The Lemon Drop Kid*. I contacted Lusk, the largest candy maker of lemon drops in the States, and thus learned much of the way of the corporate mind when two quite disparate elements were temporarily "joined at the hip" due to a mutually beneficial promotion. The old bromide of "one hand washing the other" became carved in stone for me from that early experience.

50

The author (left) with Bob Hope at a golf tournament, Palm Springs, 1950s.

*   *   *

I happily got in the habit of having a mid-morning cup of tea (served on bone china) in Audrey Hepburn's dressing room with her favorite Peek Freans tinned cookies (still "biscuits" to her). I always regretted never contacting Peek Freans in the UK regarding the promotion of a life-time supply for her while publicizing the dear girl and her latest Paramount picture at their expense.

My first involvement with Audrey actually came about when I was sent down to the LA train station to greet her on her arrival to start her contract.

Roman Holiday had not yet been released. She was still unknown and had not yet become a Hollywood phenomenon. The future movie icon was only important enough at that early date for the likes of me and one studio photographer. Her emergence as the biggest star of her time would come later. That she just happened to be a truly superb actress and a sheer delight to everyone only accentuated her appeal. Of all the countless actresses I encountered over my career, Audrey was undoubtedly my favorite. I knew our tea meetings gave her the chance to privately sound me out on publicity matters, but she did it so delightfully that I didn't care. It was so very easy to fall under her spell and I was flattered it was me she chose to be her confidant in matters PR in those very early days of her Hollywood life.

One comment on her arrival—no one knew that she would have an English boyfriend in tow. I met my first "superior than thou" public school type, and though he didn't last long in California, I often remembered him when he later became one of the wealthiest business tycoons in Britain with a title thrown in. I must say in spite of his airs, I did prefer the future Baron Hanson to Audrey's first husband, Mel Ferrer. A very difficult man, and, though unrelated, was as wrong for Audrey as his namesake, Jose Ferrer, was for his wife, Rosemary Clooney. Another of my personal favorites at Paramount, Rosie was a sweetheart to work with and was cooperative to a fault. She never became top of the tree, although the stu-

46th Street Theatre
New York, N.Y.

June 9th, 1954

My dear Jerry

I have been putting off writing until this moment to those kind people such as yourself, who wished me so well for the Academy Award. I so much wanted to do it quietly and at my leisure.

In all the excitement, your warming wishes, were the nicest part of all.

Thank you very very much.

[handwritten] Have run out of cookies, which is really the reason's am going to Europe when the play closes. Very best Audrey

Personal letter to me from Audrey Hepburn after I congratulated her on her 1954 Oscar win for *Roman Holiday.* Audrey was one of the most endearing people I've ever met (letter contents © Sean Hepburn Ferrer and Luca Dotti).

dio was certainly behind her. She did come close, but, unfortunately, film stardom is not horseshoes.

A footnote on Miss Clooney. One day a sizable number of her extended family came out to the studio for lunch and a look around. She asked me if I would give them a tour while she was at work on her set. I have often wondered if one of the young men in that family group would soon marry and one day have a Clooney named George, who today speaks with love and respect for his aunt. I, for one, endorse his feelings for a most talented and gracious lady that I found to be a pleasure in every way.

A close relation of a star I did meet was Kirk Douglas' son, Michael, when I had to see his father up at their beautiful hillside home about something or other. I remember he was a very polite twelve-year-old and did not seem to be "difficult" because his father was a famous movie star. When I met a grown Michael Douglas in Tokyo years later, I reflected that he, along with Alan Ladd, Jr., and Dick Zanuck, were all living proof that a young man, because of the accident of birth, can grow up in the rarefied air of Hollywood royalty and still turn out well-adjusted and wildly successful in his own right. No mean feat and a credit to all concerned. The many failures are as well-known as the headlines in the tabloids, but there are many whose lives reflected the fact that having a famous "name" for a parent doesn't always spell an alcohol or drug-related disaster.

* * *

There were two very big events that took place in my middle years at the studio that need mentioning. One was the 80th birthday celebration for Adolf Zukor, the Hungarian–born immigrant who founded Paramount. The party was to be, literally and figuratively, the icing on the cake of his life as one of the very first movie moguls. Little did anyone know that he would come into the New York office daily up to his one hundredth year and live for another three. The celebration was a big deal and I was quite pleased to be selected to attend to Mr. Zukor when he came out for the event. For about two weeks I was at his beck and call. I came to know what a general's aide in the army felt like after that fortnight, but no young army officer was ever privy to meeting a living history of Hollywood's elite from its earliest silent flickers days right up to the mid-fifties world of widescreen stereophonic sound.

My everlasting memory of that time was being present (sitting very quietly in a corner) at a private gathering of Zukor, Cecil B. DeMille, Jesse Lasky, and Sam Goldwyn, all major historical figures in the pantheon of Hollywood cinema's creation and development.

At a press conference a couple of days later, Vernon Scott of United Press asked, "Mister Zukor, you must have been delighted to reminisce with your fellow founders of the American Cinema?" To much laughter from the assembled crowd of media, Zukor retorted, "DeMille, Lasky, Goldwyn? They're all Johnny-come-latelies." I am sure that was the only time those historical Hollywood giants were ever referred to in such a plebeian way, but it is a fact that if Mr. Zukor didn't pre-date them all with his earlier entry into the world of nickelodeons in New York City, then he was certainly among the select few who was there at the beginning.

Of all the glitterati gathered at Paramount's largest sound stage for the birthday dinner, Mary Pickford was probably the "star of stars" and was seated next to the Birthday Boy. It was one of her very last major business-related appearances in public. I remembered this event a few years later when I had occasion to visit Pickfair, the famous home she had built with Douglas Fairbanks, and meet America's Sweetheart. But that's a story for later.

*   *   *

The other big happening was one that took place in Palm Springs at the launch of VistaVision, Paramount's widescreen answer to Fox's highly successful CinemaScope. We took over the Desert Inn Hotel and invited press from all over the country to the presentation. A few of us from publicity went up to the Springs in advance to set up all the myriad details while an army of technicians and specialists from the camera and sound departments worked with the projectionists in arranging for the all-important screening that would be the highlight of the three-day event.

The morning after arriving I had cause to be walking alone with arms full of promotional material on the spacious grounds between the giant hotel complex and the golf course. A man wearing a felt fedora (in that heat!), chinos, shirt, and desert boots was walking towards me from the private bungalows area. He stepped before me, stopped, and very politely said, "Excuse me, young man, I take it you are part of the movie activity that's taking place this weekend?" I answered in the affirmative and was shocked to realize I was standing, quite alone, face to face, with one of the world's most famous secretive and reportedly volatile personalities.

I quickly gathered my wits and politely explained what was about to happen with all the media and personalities that would be gathering there in a few days' time. The gentleman, in need of a shave, listened with interest and, ever so quietly, said, "Thank you very much, young man, you've been most helpful." I didn't expect a hundred-dollar tip to be handed my way, but all I did receive was for him to turn on his heel and walk back in the direction from whence he had suddenly appeared. As he left, I wanted to say, "You're welcome, Mister Hughes," but I didn't have the nerve to let him know I knew who he was—or that there were two beautiful young movie hopefuls among the many he had ensconced in apartments all around Los Angeles that I "knew" to the degree that Howard Hughes and I (as the old saying goes) were "kissing cousins."

Needless to say, he wasn't to be seen again while we were in Palm Springs.

* * *

A delightful set to be on was Billy Wilder's *Sabrina*, as I was very friendly with Audrey Hepburn and Bill Holden. My only concern was Humphrey Bogart, but my fears came to naught. His reputation at Warner Bros., where he had been under contract, was that of someone most difficult. I never saw that side of him. He was very professional and understood the needs of publicity people in relation to him and the film. I quickly learned that if you let him know you were not in awe of him or (God forbid!) afraid of his reaction when asked to do an interview or whatever, he was no problem. On *Sabrina*, *We're No Angels*, or *The Desperate Hours*, I never once had him turn me down when I needed his cooperation. He did tell me early on that there were one or two journalists he did not care for, and that was that. The rest all came and went with little fuss or bother.

* * *

I got to know Grace Kelly fairly well through her working on *Rear Window*, *The Bridges at Toko-Ri*, and *The Country Girl*. I found her to be friendly and always open to publicity ideas that were worthwhile. Grace did not suffer fools gladly, however, and one was on safe ground with her as long as any suggestion did not compromise her sense of position. She was very patrician in the old sense of the word and personified style. I found it took more than being well-dressed, well-coiffured, and wearing white gloves to make a lady to the manor born when I later worked with one well-known Kelly clone on a film in Paris, France. Martha Hyer had everything Grace had in looks and clothes, but, sadly, the comparison definitely ended there. Even though Miss Hyer did receive a Supporting Actress Oscar nomination for *Some Came Running*, I thought this beautiful and talented actress was fated to be a Kelly shadow.

The event that was the genesis of my eventually leaving Paramount involved Grace to a degree because she was the co-star of Hitchcock's *To Catch a Thief*, which was to have a big location in the South of France. I desperately wanted to be assigned to the film as the unit man (the publicist who works exclusively on a film while it is in production). This would have actually been a step down in the pecking order in the department for me, but I really wanted to get back to Europe, if even for a few weeks. I discussed the matter one day when enjoying a lunch out at Hitch's home. I had developed a good personal relationship with him over the years and I was flattered to be asked to meet him on a few occasions at his house in Bel Air. It was always more business-related than social, but I was still chuffed whenever asked to break bread with the Master. He said he would be happy if I was on the film, but any decision would have to come from publicity boss Norman Siegel.

In the "give and take" of studio politics, even a giant like Hitchcock would not use up a favor on a mere publicist, no matter how valued or friendly. There were so many countless never-ending day-in, day-out matters that took precedence. Favors were valuable commodities not to be wasted on the likes of me. So, though Norman agreed when the idea was first put to him, it rapidly became clear that I was not going to Cannes and Nice on location, as I was needed on other matters.

I often reflected that if I had been on *To Catch a Thief*, would I also have thought to arrange for the beautiful star to visit his private zoo and to meet the Prince of Monaco for a publicity photo-shoot? Oh well, I did go (with Arthur Jacobs) to the wedding reception. If you got it, flaunt it!

* * *

I remember like yesterday when Marlon Brando and his production company, run by his father, came to Paramount to make *One-Eyed Jacks*. I cultivated his dad and routed everything that might require Marlon's cooperation via his parent. I wasn't always successful, but I'll wager I got more publicity out of that very closed set than anyone else might have accomplished. Of course, the film went on and on and on and when the first rough assemblage of it ran some four hours, the powers that be, who had been kept at arm's length, went bananas. Didn't they know how much film was being shot, how long the film was over schedule and, most importantly, over budget? I guess his persona overwhelmed these studio execs.

Of course, they were caught between a rock and a hard place from the day the deal was signed for Brando to produce and direct his very first film (with complete carte blanche) and to be the star as well. It was really a recipe for disaster. As Joe Mankiewicz wrote in his screenplay of *All About Eve*— "It's going to be a bumpy ride."

One-Eyed Jacks was not the unmitigated catastrophe several years later of UA's *Heaven's Gate*—but it certainly left in its wake a few very bruised and battered Paramount executive reputations. The New York big brass were famous for being horrified whenever they encountered their two most hated and feared words in the English language—"over budget." I guess all concerned were taken in by the "emperor's clothes"! However, Brando more than made up for his *One-Eyed Jacks* debacle by playing Don Corleone for the studio a decade later. And who knows?—perhaps *Jacks* would have been better had Brando not fired the original director, Stanley Kubrick, when the project was just getting off the ground.

* * *

A tragic happening took place late in the filming of *My Son John*, directed by the great Hollywood veteran Leo McCarey. Its lead, Robert Walker (first husband of Jennifer Jones), died from his body's massive rejection to a prescribed sedative to calm his never-ending nervousness. A double, an amazing look-alike, who caused quite a stir the first day he came in the commissary for lunch, was used for the long and medium shots needed to help bridge certain action necessary to finish the film.

The death scene at the end of the script became the big stumbling block. It was solved by Alfred Hitchcock, who allowed his footage of Walker's death at the end of *Strangers on a Train* to be used by his good friend McCarey. The special effects/photographic people skillfully made this work and inserted the Hitchcock frames into the final hospital scene as required. This was decades before the magic of computer graphics. McCarey doubled as Walker's voice for the few lines of needed dialogue. How very unusual for an actor to dramatically die in the same footage in two different films and for real during one of them!

Paramount—A Director of TV/ Radio

I knew that my days at Paramount would end sooner than later so hopefully with luck and perseverance I would be able to decide when this was to be. I let Norman know of my disappointment that the French location no-no and the small raise in salary did little to mollify my frustration at the situation.

Thoughts of leaving were somewhat compromised when another step up the ladder came about when one of the "plum jobs" in the Publicity Department opened up. Prior to my getting this somewhat prized position there had been but two others before me with the title of director of TV/radio. One left to become the first Editor of *TV Weekly* and the other to become the publisher of the major English language paper in Mexico City. It sounded very grand but this was at a time that TV represented little more than another platform to promote the company's feature films. I was to become instrumental in developing the whole concept of the behind the scenes coverage and also the off-set star interview when the personality was filmed answering a set of questions. The local TV interviewer could be added by cutting in the film by the local TV station so it would appear to be a live interview. As a result, I can honestly say that I have "directed" Alfred Hitchcock—with whom we did one of these potted interviews for *Rear Window*.

The principal activity of the TV/radio department was taking actors to shows produced at the West Coast studios of the three main networks based in LA, namely CBS, NBC, and ABC. The big comedy shows featuring the likes of Jack Benny, George Gobel, Burns and Allen, *The Colgate Comedy Hour*, and others. Lucille Ball's Desilu was at RKO (she was soon to own the entire plant) and I particularly recall the fun Bill Holden had when he appeared in one of the episodes of *I Love Lucy*. He said it was one of the most enjoyable filming experiences in his career up to that time. Also, most interesting was when the big East Coast–like TV stars came out to LA to do a few shows there. I particularly remember Ed Sullivan from when we flew up to San Francisco in a small twin-engine Piper aircraft for him to do a sequence with Bing Crosby, who was at his beautiful home near Pebble Beach. We arrived after dark in changing weather that made for a hairy couple of hours. I remarked to Sullivan that I thought of the headline, "Ed Sullivan and Unidentified Friend Missing on LA to San Francisco Flight." He wasn't amused, even though we had already landed!

My most personally rewarding association from this time was when Edward R. Murrow did his famous *Person to Person* with a couple of our stars. Bing Crosby was a particular rating success for him and resulted in my being invited to a private lunch the next time I was in New York. When it finally happened, it became one of my favorite memories. Even though I was always associating with "stars," there is always someone more "stellar" in the firmament of life. Murrow had a magical persona of greatness.

Paramount enjoyed a close association with *Lux Video Theatre* due to the long tenure of Cecil B. DeMille with the defunct *Lux Radio Theatre* of the thirties and fourtis. Many of our scripts were adapted, so I was very often with the Lux people. James Mason was the host and I found him very hard going. He still thought he was Britain's Number One screen actor.

Of all our stars who did his or her "thing" on TV to promote their films, I found Mitzi Gaynor one of the most cooperative, and Doris Day one of the least. She never ever helped promote a film, even *The Man Who Knew Too Much*. Co-composer Jay Livingstone told me she didn't particularly like her song "Que Sera, Que Sera." Later when it became one of her very biggest hits, all those earlier problems seemed to be forgotten, but still no promotion. Another lesson in the foibles of fame.

Paramount—Hope Is Eternal

The evolvement of my relationship with Bob Hope took many twists and turns over most of the fifties. I became one of his extended show-business family and, though the studio paid my salary, I found myself working for Bob on many levels. I accompanied many of his shows visiting military or naval facilities in the States, but never to Korea or other overseas places. I went in advance to help arrange all PR matters. This led to another interesting facet of this time with Bob. He had a set routine that involved humorous but rather caustic comments on certain officers in the unit, ship, or a base concerned. These pithy "put-downs" guaranteed a very raucous in house laugh at the officer's expense. The enlisted men loved it! I would research the names of the officers most likely to guarantee a laugh and slot them into the pre-written jokes. This slowly led to my sitting-in on several of the writers' meetings with Bob and his large team of very funny scribblers, and this soon evolved into a private deal with Bob. If I wrote a joke that he liked, he paid me a small amount (not small to me!). If he actually used the gag, I got double! This happened three or four times, so I can honestly say I wrote jokes for Hope—although I was most certainly never one of his official writers.

When he started his cerebral palsy charity shows, he asked the studio to loan me to his team to head up the publicity. This also brought me closer to Jerry Lewis, who at this time first became interested in what was to become his lifelong stewardship of the U.S. charity fund-raising to combat the dreaded children's disease. I liked Lewis very much and he was always very friendly whenever I was on one of his sets or meeting for an interview at lunch in the studio commissary.

It is impossible to mention Jerry Lewis in those days without saying something about Dean Martin. Okay, I've said something! The only time I ever saw Dean truly content was during the location filming of *The Caddy*, when he could practice his swing between takes out at the exclusive Los Angeles Country Club location. When it came to personality, I found Martin to be as taciturn as Lewis was terrific. I must say, though, that talent-wise I always felt that Martin was underrated and I was not too surprised that his later solo career outshone and outlasted Lewis. Be that as it may, Jerry Lewis' great talent was only matched by his warmth and humanity. A genuinely nice guy whose illness became a major factor in cutting short his glittering career.

A footnote on Hope. When I left the studio, Bob said we would stay in touch and my time with him in France certainly proved his comment prophetic.

Paramount—A Potpourri

I remember one day when the Hal Wallis company publicity director, Walter Seltzer, brought over to the table by the left wall in the commissary, where the publicity people always ate, one Elvis Presley. He had just signed a contract with our most successful producer. Wallis, who was a great force in Hollywood, had been responsible for some of the greatest hits at Warner Bros. during its glory days. Presley was so polite, gracious, and soft-spoken that it was almost impossible to connect him to the person supposedly corrupting young American womanhood with his hip-swiveling, crotch-forward singing style. He was, in one word, a delight.

Another visitor to our table was a very pretty and voluptuous Swiss miss who spoke little English but was quite something to behold in the flesh. She wasn't signed, but it was a first encounter with Ursula Andress.

To remain in the commissary for a moment, I'll long treasure the memory of the first lunch when Clark Gable walked in. He had come to co-star with Doris Day and the delightful Gig Young in *Teacher's Pet*. He was "The

King" and the never-ending buzz of conversation came to a thundering halt at His Majesty's arrival. Quite an amazing moment, as a large roomful of industry workers momentarily were turned into "fans."

A few names I came to know during my Hollywood sojourn include the Danish tenor Lauritz Melchior, whose hilltop home featured more mounted heads of dead animals on every wall than the mythical Trader Horn. Another actor I came to know from evenings around the watering holes of the Sunset Strip was Michael Rennie, the suave English leading man (*The Day the Earth Stood Still*) and a super ladies' man on film and for real.

I always remembered my mother whenever I would come across the old silent star Jack Mulhall, as he was without a doubt her favorite screen personality.

At one point on some charity show, I briefly had to deal with the two great song and dance men, Dan Dailey and Donald O'Connor. This meant visits out to Fox. It was always interesting when matters had me at other studios as a working visitor. I forget the details but I had to go out to the Valley to do some promotion or other with the 1940s star George Montgomery. He ran a successful carpentry business at the time, but I found him of interest because of two reasons. One, he had starred as a trumpet player in the Glenn Miller Band in one of my all-time favorite films, *Orchestra Wives*. The other was because he was the ex-husband of the great singing star Dinah Shore. Back in my military school days she sang with the Nashville Tennessee Orchestra of one Charles Nagy at our dances. In those days she was known not as Dinah, but by the more pedestrian and very Deep South name of Fanny Rose.

*   *   *

Many foreign stars passed through the lot over the years; a few I remember meeting and dealing with include the British Peter Ustinov, Deborah Kerr, Glynis Johns, Cecil Parker, and John Williams, Audrey Hepburn's father in *Sabrina* and the detective in *To Catch a Thief*. The Teutonic contingent was led by Otto Preminger, Marlene Dietrich, Sig Ruman, and Werner Klemperer. Several French names include Claude Dauphin, Jean-Pierre Aumont, Marcel Dalio, and the sweet Nicole Maurey. A Dane I came to know well was producer Frederick Brisson, the husband of star Rosalind Russell. When they came to Paramount to make *The Girl Rush*, I became quite involved with them and seemed to spend an inordinate amount of time on that film right up through distribution. Brisson was demanding, but as long as I was in favor with Rosalind (and I made sure I was!), all went well. In the late forties he was known at Warner Bros. as "The Lizard of Roz." I never found him that bad, but he was no one to cross!

The studio production heads were always happy when an employee was in favor with a star, as they became a valuable informant of what was going on and could also be of great help as a go-between if necessary. A publicist became of extra value if this relationship developed, and in my six years, I milked this for as much as I could! I remember well that our best female publicist was practically joined at the hip to Betty Hutton, a lady of many moods!

A very sweet Irish lass, Audrey Dalton, is also especially remembered, as is the Canadian Suzanne Cloutier. Our "Latin Lovers" were represented by Fernando Lamas and that very model of film longevity, Gilbert Roland. I came to know him rather well because of countless Sunday trips to Tijuana on the Mexican border for the bullfights during the season. The excursions became quite the social occasions, and being there with Roland (son of a matador) didn't hurt one bit in being part of the Hollywood in-crowd when it came to the *Fiesta Brava*.

I cannot think of those halcyon days (before the Mexican border became a drug-fueled war zone) without remembering one of our Golden Circle beauties, Ann Robinson, who was quite the "aficionada" of both the bulls and those very ballsy *toreros*, who fought them on those long-ago afternoons of "Blood and Sand." She had made her name as co-star with Gene Barry in *The War of the Worlds*—and I do mean the original 1953 version and not the later Tom Cruise over-the-top hokum. Our epic was the brainchild of the Hungarian-born George Pal, a sci-fi genius. George was one of the nicest people you could ever hope to know. His great producing talent was never given the credit it deserved. He was truly one of those who was ahead of his time and was a sweetheart of a man greatly admired by his contemporaries. He did win multiple Oscars for his many special effects innovations over the years.

A very American actress has to be included in this list. Though I never met Gloria Grahame during the filming of *The Greatest Show on Earth*, I was responsible for exclusively handling her when we were promoting the pre-release campaign for the film in Los Angeles. Gloria was quite unique in that the extreme sexuality she exuded on film was very much part of her real-life persona. In one word—she was just "overwhelming."

* * *

The proximity of Los Angeles to Las Vegas meant that the occasional weekend in the then relatively early days of the gambling mecca of the Western World was easy to achieve. A couple of hours drive was a small price to pay for a complete break to recharge the batteries.

One particular event that needs mentioning came about when I was checking into the Flamingo Hotel (one of the four in Vegas then) and encountered Al Horwits, one of the legendary newspapermen who came to Hollywood to be a publicist. He went on to become a big wheel at Columbia. He called out to me and then explained that one of his guests was unable to make it—was I free to join his group for the dinner-show? I sure was, and that night I found myself sitting at a table with, of all people, Al's good friend, one Ernest Hemingway. I told him of our brief encounter at the Scribe Hotel in Paris and then sat quietly with the others through dinner listening to his stories of sports, hunting, places, women, and whatever!

The headliner of the show was the newly "arrived" singing star Johnny Mathis. As he was performing, his first numbers in his near-falsetto singing style, the very macho Hemingway motioned to us and leaned forward to whisper to the seven of us, conspiratorially, "I just might not integrate!"

*   *   *

Of all the films made at the studio while I was there, one of the very best had to be the George Stevens classic *Shane*, starring Alan Ladd in the best role of his career, Van Heflin, the venerable Jean Arthur, the young Brandon De Wilde, and Jack Palance as the hired gun in a villainous performance that made him a star. The scene where he literally blows Elisha Cook, Jr., off his feet by a few well-paced revolver shots electrified audiences everywhere. Cook, who built a career out of being killed by Humphrey Bogart in Warner Bros. films, never was dispatched so graphically. The bar room fight became a classic of screen violence choreography. If ever stuntmen should have been recognized for excellence, it was for *Shane*.

I have mentioned the best. The worst had to be one of the monumental turkeys in major studio history, *Aaron Slick from Punkin Crick*. The title should have been enough to warn all the makers off the project. The rumor around the lot was that the book was a favorite of the studio head's wife, Mrs. Freeman. After all these years, I still can't get my head round why this nonsense was ever made. I can only imagine the reaction when it was first screened by the sales and pub/ad people in New York. We at the studio never talked about that film, even among ourselves.

Paramount—Back to the Future

In 2013, while on a trip to Southern California, I decided to drive over to visit my old stomping grounds of some sixty years before. The once familiar buildings of Paramount Pictures Studio were either gone or so remodeled and/or replaced as to make the outside of the plant almost unrecognizable. It was a totally different vista from the one I once knew like the back of my hand.

As I briefly parked my rented Chevrolet near the giant wrought-iron gate, the iconic symbol of the studio and the only unchanged feature from my time there, I was suddenly haunted by the "ghosts of pictures past!" Like Dickens' Scrooge, I, too, had visions, mine of long gone faces, once known around the world.

Driving around the perimeter of Paramount with the giant billboards announcing upcoming releases, my reverie continued as DiCaprio, Diaz, and Cruise morphed into Holden, Hepburn, and Crosby.

As I swung onto Melrose Avenue to head west back toward my Beverly Hills hotel, I was suddenly filled with a great sadness. I was like Proust, trying to recapture the taste of some long ago eaten cupcake. As some other old guy once famously said—*sic transit gloria mundi* ("there goes the glory of the world").

APJAC

Much time passed during which I was considered for various positions that might result in my leaving. Some decided I wasn't right for them and I felt a few weren't right for me. I particularly remember meeting the publicity director for Goldwyn Films and then with the great man himself in his office. Also with the Hecht-Hill-Lancaster Company, one of the biggest of the independents. Of course, I knew Burt from his many films made at Paramount. I was briefly interim vice president of the Screen Publicists Guild, so I was one of the speakers at that year's annual "Panhandle Dinner" for the Hollywood media. After six years, I was becoming better known as not just another studio hack.

I should mention before taking my leave of Hollywood that I was put forward for membership in the Academy of Motion Pictures Arts and Sciences during my last two years at Paramount. I was seconded and accepted and was issued membership number 5005. I later thought that it would have been another prophetic coincidence if my number had been two entries later, but I guess one can't have everything.

One day I got a call from Arthur P. Jacobs, head of his own highly successful public relations firm. I had already been over to Rogers and Cowan, who together ran the other major independent publicity firm in Hollywood. Between them, APJAC and R&C handled just about every major motion picture personality. I met with Arthur, and it ended with his asking if I was interested in joining his company with my first account being the handling of his client, Marilyn Monroe, and her newly formed production company headed by her partner Milton Greene, the well-known New York fashion photographer. They were soon starting production of her first independent film, then called *The Sleeping Prince*, with Sir Laurence Olivier directing and co-starring. The icing on the cake for me was that production would be in London for a minimum of four months. I was definitely interested and duly went out to Fox with Arthur to meet the sex goddess of the Western World in her sumptuous dressing room so she could decide if she "liked the cut of my jib." I passed muster and was offered the job. This was in early March 1956 and the advance plans meant that we would have to duly leave for England via New York in late June.

Not realizing my life, both professionally and personally, was about to change forevermore, I returned to my office and immediately called Siegel for a meeting. It was difficult to tell the man who brought me to Hollywood that I was leaving, but I had given him six years of hard and loyal work. I did remind him of my big disappointment over the *To Catch a Thief* French location business and my having told him then that I wasn't going to stay at the studio forever. Norman said he wasn't surprised and was well aware of my looking around over the past months. Anyway, it was all friendly enough and Norman gave me my leave (nothing had ever been in writing). I left Paramount for Arthur's up-market Beverly Hills office.

Arthur wanted to take me with him to Europe earlier than planned, as he was handling the press for his client's upcoming wedding. The client was Grace Kelly, with the nuptials taking place in Monte Carlo for her marriage to Prince Rainier of Monaco. There was also a film on location in Monte Carlo that he was handling that featured a certain young actress he was rather anxious to see. Natalie Trundy, a beautiful and talented blonde from New York, would later become Mrs. Arthur Jacobs.

Before leaving LA, I had to fit in a meeting with another one of Jacob's clients, Esther Williams. She had organized a big aquatic-themed (what else?) show with dozens of swimmers and divers. She would be opening her tour in London in the late summer, so Arthur decided that, separate to my primary duties with Monroe, I would have to find time to handle PR for Williams.

We were to spend a full week in New York. There were to be visits to the film set of the successful play, *12 Angry Men*, the first motion picture of stage director Sidney Lumet. It was a "work of love" with little upfront money for star Henry Fonda in order to get the picture green lit. There were also necessary meetings with the top publicity people at Warner Bros.'s New York office, as that company was releasing the Monroe movie. The Warners meetings showed me a whole new facet of the world of the business of motion pictures. At the studio, the emphasis was on production—getting the picture made as close to budget as possible was the order of the day. Those employed in the world of distribution/sales (in the U.S. this primarily meant New York) had only one mantra—how much was to be spent on creating the campaign and on the launching. The question of a given film being successful enough to return the company's investment, perhaps be a box office success, and go into profit was all that mattered. These were the days before what are now called "ancillary rights." The big return was from world cinema distribution. New films were not sold for repeated TV showings, and the sales of videocassettes, DVDs, Blu-ray, and streaming were all in the future. Soundtrack records were not considered of financial importance except for helping to sell the film. Everything was centered on the first releases and it was a rare film that survived a poor opening couple of weeks. A few years later I was to be central to one of the biggest exceptions to that rule—namely United Artists' handling of *Dr. No*, the first James Bond film.

The Prince and the Showgirl (the final title of the picture originally called *The Sleeping Prince*) was to be a major factor in Warners' plans for the following season, so Arthur and I were treated reasonably well. It was a fact that while the pub/ad department of a distribution company had one aim—the successful release of the film—an independent publicity company was usually interested only in the fortunes of the star who employed its service. The exception to this was when the PR company was also signed (and well paid) to help organize and to co-oversee the release campaign. When that was the case, the mutual interest in a film's success was equal, so everyone had to be reasonably cooperative and friendly.

More often than not, a New York head office publicity and advertising department had to accept (as a necessary evil?) a private PR firm's personnel if they were representing the interests of the independent company producing the film. After all, they were central to the talent (their paymaster) being available and willing to do what was considered to be in the best interest of all concerned. Easier said than done!

Arthur and I were in and out of many meetings at Warners while also visiting the set of *12 Angry Men*, a production being handled by APJAC. After one has spent a few years on film sets, it would be logical to think that there would be some spark that might indicate a big success in the works, much less an iconic happening or the launch of a new genre of filmmaking. I confess I got no such vibes during my observations of the work of the actors in that very hot and sweaty jury room set in lower Manhattan. No individual scene or two will ever reflect the final finished work of the director, film editor, or others who contribute to a brilliant and successful product.

I also didn't take into account the magic of Henry Fonda's underplaying style that became powerful in the extreme when actually seen on the big screen. Fonda and Gregory Peck were masters of this technique of acting, and their many awards are testament to this fact. One actor who never achieved such accolades but was one of the greatest practitioners of the art of acting for the screen was Robert Mitchum, who should certainly be in the top ten of anyone's list of all the great motion picture actors with emphasis on the words "motion picture."

Among the so-called character actors, none ever topped Claude Raines, who made standing quietly, while seemingly watching the other actors "act," into an art form. His work in *Casablanca* is for me one of the greatest ever examples of this no longer seen expertise.

One day Arthur told me we were going to a party at Leonard Bernstein's midtown apartment; a couple of his clients would be there and was the reason for the invite. A possible project that could involve APJAC was to be initially discussed at some point during the evening. Anyway, it was all very grand with Judy Garland (no less!), songwriters Comden and Greene, and an "in-group" who didn't feel awed in the presence of America's most famous home-grown maestro/composer. Among the many famous New York thespians present, I particularly remember Celeste Holm, a most delightful lady.

After some ten days in the luxury of a suite in the Sherry-Netherland Hotel (Arthur's New York favorite), we took off on a Pan Am Constellation for London. First class seats and sleeper beds and meals in an upper-deck dining room with candelabra, damask linen, and silver cutlery. Ah, those innocent airline days of yore before the big-time problems of the 21st century. As for me, I quickly became accustomed to the luxuries of life with the Jacobs company, where the client was charged for everything.

Life with Marilyn

After the bright modern airport terminals of Los Angeles and New York, it was something of a culture shock to land in London in the year 1956 and find large Quonset-type huts from the World War II era serving as the arrival halls. There was still a certain laid-back innocence to life in the UK, old fashioned values that would finally change in the Swinging Sixties. This was the world in which the Monroe Productions advance team found itself. What was very evident, however, was that the world's most famous sex symbol was perhaps an even larger personality in the UK than in the States.

At our first meetings with Olivier, I obviously never mentioned our last encounter during Leigh's LA departure. We got along from the start as I did remind him of the *Sister Carrie* days at Paramount and that I was there in London as much for his best interests as that of Monroe. When later on push came to shove, I was on his side and he knew it. However, via Greene and Jacobs, I always covered myself with the Monroe camp so that my best efforts were always on behalf of the picture and its eventual box office success. That was truly my position, but I was not about to let my loyalty to Milton and Arthur color my position of cooperation and friendly interaction with our director/co-star. In my decades of work in the film industry, this was the only time I had to walk such a tightrope when one misstep meant a fall from which there was no immediate recovery. Many years later when I was with United Artists in Europe and had to be involved with *Khartoum*, both in the UK and at the Egyptian location, Olivier did say how much he appreciated my efforts to be neutral during that traumatic summer of '56.

It soon became abundantly clear to us that Monroe's arrival was akin to knowing a hurricane was approaching. All the facts and figures showed the big storm to be inevitable. One could only prepare as best one could, to ride it out and hopefully come out in one piece. That analogy roughly captures the eye of the storm in which I found myself as the point man with regard to the British and European media gathering for The Arrival!

Her very recent marriage to the famous American playwright Arthur Miller only added to the mounting hysteria, and I for one was very happy when they finally arrived. Reality can be faced; the unknown is always diffi-

69

cult. A slightly nervous Olivier was at the airport to greet her and that was followed the next day by a very successful press conference at the Savoy Hotel. All of us breathed a sigh of relief! This was to be my personal apogee of employer–employee friendliness and happiness, chez Marilyn Monroe Productions, Inc. The workplace of Pinewood Studios was soon to become a battle

The author escorting Marilyn Monroe from her very first British press conference for Warner Bros.' *The Prince and the Showgirl*, Savoy Hotel, London, 1956. Her then-husband Arthur Miller is far left.

zone in the long, long weeks to come. It was the last time that I found myself to be in complete favor with Monroe. Truly, the press gathering was a big success, not because of my organizational handling, but because of her wit, charm and intelligence in turning the oh-so-cynical British show business press from big jungle cats, ready to pounce on a helpless prey, into little kittens somewhat hypnotized by her mesmerizing magic.

When one was on the set and watched Marilyn do a scene, you saw movement and heard dialogue, but nothing that caused goose bumps. But!—in the screening room, when seeing the rushes, it was something else. By some mysterious process of osmosis, between the live action, the camera's lens, the film, the processing, and then the projection onto a screen, something somewhere in all that—magic happened! What you saw on the set was not what you observed in the screening room. I will never know the answer because I'm not sure there is one. This charisma was what audiences all over the world paid for and saw from their cinema seats. This was what, for those years as Queen of the Hill, set her very much apart and kept her at the pinnacle of the Hollywood Heap.

When the Savoy Hotel press conference ended we (Monroe, Miller and *moi*) slowly walked through endless people until we found ourselves finally in the grand lobby approaching the revolving front door. I suddenly saw Ava Gardner, very casually dressed with little makeup, starting to enter from the street side. She saw Monroe and the approaching horde of photographers coming from within and continued going around in the revolving door and went back out without ever entering the hotel. No one else noticed her, as all eyes were on Marilyn. Ava must have been relieved not to have got caught up in what would have been one of the major photos in the press the next day, a somewhat disheveled Gardner being upstaged by the perfectly coiffed and dressed Monroe.

The next night I was accompanying Marilyn (as Miller was somewhere or other doing his thing) to a screening at the 20th Century–Fox office in Soho Square. As the limo pulled to a stop, she turned to me and said, "Jerry, you did a good job at the press conference," and leaned over and kissed me on the cheek. That moment was to be the last warmth in my time with her. From that point on it was all downhill.

It is impossible to try and give any kind of chronological order to those months, so I'll list a few random happenings that affected me personally.

An American producer resident in London invited Marilyn and any entourage she cared to bring to a showing of his latest film, starring, if memory serves, Alan Ladd. A few of us went to the screening room in Audley Square and I met for the first time, Albert R. "Cubby" Broccoli. How was I to know this man would one day in a few years' time become the center of my life? All I remember of that first meeting was that he had known Monroe from her early days in Hollywood and had been a good friend of then fellow agent Johnny Hyde, her great protector, lover, and advisor. I am sure Hyde's sudden death was certainly one of many contributory factors to her fragility.

Before too long, life on the film became unbearable. I found I could not recommend or offer any suggestion or give an opinion because her mindset became such that whatever I suggested was inevitably never in her best interest. She was certain that there had to be an ulterior motive that was to be for my benefit, not hers. One cannot work under such a condition for long, so survival became the name of the game. In fact, I was privately offered $5000 (no small amount then) by someone at the famous French magazine *Paris Match* if I got her to Paris for a weekend. I never considered this because even though in fact it would have been great publicity, it would also have been a fiasco. To get her there in the first place, plus the demands on her time, it would never have worked!

Between Miller, one of the most difficult people I've ever encountered, and Paula Strasberg, wife of Actors Studio guru Lee Strasberg and the lady I called the "Wicked Witch of the East," I very quickly found myself the one American from the Monroe camp who was on the side of Olivier. Believe it or not, some of the Monroe inner circle put the seed in her mind that Olivier was out to destroy her career.

This greatest English-speaking actor and superb prize-winning director was, after all was said and done, in her company's employ, but Marilyn's paranoia and persecution complex knew no bounds. She and her close entourage (led by Strasberg) made his life hell on and off the set, and this lovely man was practically brought to his knees by this psychologically challenged, most famous woman in the world.

One night during production, at about 3 in the morning, my London phone rang. I sleepily answered to hear the urgency in Milton Greene's voice. He told me to get to his house (just off South Audley Street and only a few minutes from my Upper Brook Street flat). Some fifteen minutes later, we were in Milton's car, driving westward toward TROUBLE! Arthur Miller had called Milton to say he had phoned an ambulance to take a comatose Marilyn to a local medical facility. We arrived to find that "Miss Baker" had already been pumped out and was recovering in a private room. Our star was on call for filming at Pinewood in a few hours' time, and it was obvious she wouldn't just be late, she wouldn't be there at all.

However, on that "star-crossed" production, what was another hundred thousand dollars or so to a cost sheet already way over budget.

From my standpoint, that eventful night was not all bad, as not one single word of it ever appeared in the media. No typical London tabloid banners screamed "Marilyn in Death Dash" etc., ad nauseam. Those British medical practitioners of the fifties respected the privacy of those they were attending. However, if Milton passed around a few well placed "tips," they never knew and didn't want to!

It was, however, an exhausting few hours, and the title of the Beatles' song/film of a few years in the future perfectly captured what for me had truly been a "hard day's night."

* * *

I managed to keep the degree of bitterness that developed between Monroe and Olivier out of the British press, even though our British unit publicist was fired after writing a behind-the-scenes story for one of the Sunday papers on some of what was really happening at dear old Pinewood Studios in leafy idyllic Buckinghamshire. Despite that, Milton Greene, who was "Piggy in the Middle," did appreciate what the publicity department was accomplishing. That he kept his sanity and laid-back charm was a miracle, and I held him in high esteem. The Milton Greene I knew was a talented and caring person, and I valued his friendship. His tenure at the head of Marilyn Monroe Productions was not to last long, though, certainly longer than mine. His very early death a few years later was a great loss.

At the end of production, I returned to the States with Jacobs and saw out my duties on *The Prince and the Showgirl* when required. I continued working in concert with the New York publicity department of Warner Bros., particularly during the New York premiere. The most traumatic happening during that time was when Warners decided they needed a specially posed photo of Monroe and Olivier for the advertising campaign. I had to fly to London and accompany a very reluctant Larry to New York. We left the hotel to go to Greene's studio where Olivier put on his costume, a polka-dotted silk robe. Madame arrived and after the briefest of greetings the session started. Two rolls of film later—only some twenty shots—our diva said, "That's it!" and left. As the saying goes, that was that! One of those few frames fortunately was used for the campaign, but it was all somewhat in vain because the reviews and lack of box office success quickly brought my work on the film to an end.

I do remember, however, the premiere in New York when my presence was hardly acknowledged by her, a long way from the night of the Royal Command Performance in London the previous year when I was practically glued to her side—Miller on the other—to get her through the "scrum," both in the cinema and the outer lobby, as we left to try and get to the limo waiting in Leicester Square. The London bobbies that night would have got an early taste of the fan madness that was to become so commonplace in the soon to come rock 'n' roll star hysteria years of the sixties.

When Marilyn accepted the invitation to be one of the stars to be presented to Her Majesty the Queen at the 1956 Royal Command Performance, my principal focus was no longer the film but rather her eventual appearance on the night. Everyone knew that protocol demanded that at any and all functions the Queen was the last to arrive, and as Monroe was pathologically challenged to arrive anywhere on time, it all became my sole concern and took over my life. For example, as she was too busy filming, I had to represent her at the rehearsal of the star lineup and then report back what was expected. The presence of a publicist in her place became something of a *cause célèbre*. My fifteen minutes of fame was standing in for Marilyn Monroe. At least I didn't have to wear a dress, which is a great segue to what follows.

One memorable day I had to go to the atelier of the film's famed wardrobe designer, great character, and old Olivier hand, Beatrice "Bumble" Dawson, who was designing and making the figure-hugging (what else?) white dress that was to be worn on the night. I went to Bumble's workshop in London, where I was introduced to an elderly gentleman who was taking tea with her. She said, "Jerry, this is Clive Brook." I was almost speechless. As a film buff, I was bowled over to meet the great British leading man of the twenties and thirties, to whom one of the most iconic lines in the history of motion pictures was said when Marlene Dietrich purred, "It took more than one man to change my name to Shanghai Lily" (*Shanghai Express*). I might have been working for Marilyn Monroe on a daily basis, but "WOW"—to meet Clive Brook! I guess what represents fame is surely in the eyes of the beholder.

One momentous encounter I had with our star toward the end of filming must be mentioned. I was called over to her dressing room, and when I arrived she was in her white terry cloth robe with nothing else covering the "world's most desirable woman." The belted robe was as open as it was closed, and subconsciously or not, this was her way of saying loud and clear—"You are my employee and a very lowly placed one at that; plus, you do not represent a man to me; you are a meaningless thing that exists only for my needs here at work." No Russian aristocrat in Tsarist Russia could have interrelated with his lowly serf/servant more clearly than was done with me at that time.

* * *

Arrangements were being finalized for the departure back to New York and it took all the persuasive powers of Jacobs, plus the head of Warner Bros. production in the UK and myself, to persuade Olivier that he had to be at Heathrow to be photographed giving Monroe a "going away present" of a beautiful watch. Naturally, it was charged to the film's overhead. It is a little short of amazing what so often ends up on a film's budget that has so little to do with what ends up on the screen!

Before taking my leave from London Town I must mention that when the Esther Williams Show came over, I had to hire a small staff to do most of the work and all went well. I liked Esther and we got along famously. It didn't hurt that I got a full-page photo in *Life* Magazine for her. It showed a couple of elderly cleaning ladies doing a "knees-up" as they watched from backstage the pool-side musical number being performed by Esther's bathing beauties. I had covered myself with Greene by telling him of "this other duty" and I wouldn't allow it to interfere with my main job on *Prince*. The secret of success for those who worked at a private showbiz PR firm was to be able to juggle! What I didn't tell Milton was that I felt my few visits down to the Williams venue was akin to going from the zoo to the botanical gardens.

Marilyn Finis

Regarding the 2011 film *My Week with Marilyn*, my comments relate to what happened as I remember it. However, it is a drama, not a documentary. First, Michelle Williams did a very good job. Her Oscar and BAFTA nominations speak volumes. She became Marilyn, although the screenplay had her being too "misunderstood." None of the underlying real-life hardness shone through the outward fragility. Kenneth Branagh was very good as Olivier, but I never once saw Larry blow up in frustration on the set. In private, yes, but never in front of the cast and/or crew. As for Milton Greene, never can I imagine him saying he had slept with Marilyn as he does in the film, and certainly not to a third assistant director who may or may not have become important to the scheme of things—primarily Monroe's fractured psyche that made her compulsively late or unable to show up at all.

Dame Judi Dench had been asked (by the script) to play Dame Sybil Thorndyke as too favorable to Marilyn, but I do accept the dramatic necessity as a balance to Olivier's abrasiveness and frustration resulting from Monroe's traumas. Not that anyone cares, but because such attention went into the casting of the rest of the principals, I found that the actor playing Arthur Jacobs was over the top. I shudder to think how I might have been portrayed if I had been considered important enough. Sometimes it pays to be Number Two!

In reality when the "week" in question actually took place, Jacobs was back in the States and I was never brought into the loop on this particular occasion. After all, why should one week be different from any other on such a "happy" set? Having said all that—a very personal and jaundiced insider viewpoint, I admit—I thought it was a good film, well told and surprisingly authentic in the recreation of time and place. For me, seeing it was like a trip to the Twilight Zone as I sat in my seat in a small cinema off Baker Street. I really was transported back to Pinewood Studios of 1956.

A mention of Colin Clark, who wrote the book upon which the movie was based. That I have no memory of him on the production proves nothing, as there are countless people in a film company who are interrelated only by the nature of their work, ranking, and, often on an international production, nationality. I am equally sure he has no memory of me. I certainly never came across him in my office in the main building at Pinewood or down the hall in the production office, a place to stay away from whenever possible so there was little chance of getting to know anyone in that environment of controlled chaos. Certainly not a third assistant director about as low on the food chain on a film production as one can get. Remember, we're talking over fifty years ago, when egality was not the flavor of the month. Finally, as for whether Clark actually went to bed with Monroe, which the script so craftily leaves open to conjecture, I defer to the French phrase with all its Gallic shades of meaning, *sait-on jamais* (who knows?)—and really, who cares?

A final thought. If *I* were to write only of that summer of 1956, I can only think of one title that truly captured the spirit of what transpired, but I have a strong feeling it has already been used—*Star Wars!*

* * *

In spite of everything, from the perspective of time, I am grateful for having been part of Marilyn's Magical Mystery Tour for a brief period and I do thank her if the use of her name in the title helps to sell this book that you, dear reader, now have open before you. Also, I must admit that for the rest of my career (such as it was), it never failed to cause a ripple whenever I had cause to mention my time with Marilyn Monroe. I guess it's a bit like being a veteran of the Wehrmacht who had been at the siege of Stalingrad, somehow survived, and was forever able to say he had been there through the blood, sweat, and tears. Maybe not a fair analogy, but I think my meaning is clear.

It would be most hypocritical of me if I didn't acknowledge that, in spite of everything, my time spent with Marilyn is right at the top of my curriculum vitae. Looking back on my life in the film business, Monroe and Bond head any list of credits without a doubt.

The respected British writer Leo McKinstry wrote a newspaper article for the London *Daily Mail* on Monroe prior to the release of the 2011 film. It was a well-studied assessment of his take on Monroe and what made her the way she was. He wrote (quite correctly) that her early (almost inevitable) death was an accident. He felt (and I agree) all other conspiracy theories are nonsense. I once discussed this with my former Jacob's PR colleague, Pat Newcomb, who was there in LA still handling her when it all came to a world's headline-making end. I am convinced, for what it is still worth, that she died by her own actions, intended or not. Whatever demons congregated to cause it we will never really know, though there will always be conjecture as long as there remain those who remember. I will comment later on a happening on the news of her death that took place when I was with United Artists and had Peter Sellers, Nanette Newman, and her director husband, Bryan Forbes, visiting our Paris apartment. It was an incredibly traumatic moment which I will explain.

If I had been McKinstry, I would have ended the piece as follows—"When all is said and done, she was a quixotic combination of doubt, fear, and uncertainty mixed with power, fame, and talent. It was this talent for acting, whether learned or inherent, that enabled little old Norma Jeane Mortenson from Northern California to grow up and become an actress to play, for better or for worse, her greatest role—that of the world-famous movie star named Marilyn Monroe."

To close these thoughts on the diva Monroe, I will just say that she was a unique but enigmatic star, and that I would do it all again in a flash if possible. In spite of the trauma and angst, I was certainly *alive* for those months at ground zero of the film world working for its most beautiful and famous film producer ever.

Lynn

This seems to be as good a place as any to bring up something that occurred during this period of my life that is right up there—certainly more significant—than meeting any so-called "star."

Lunch in the beautiful oak-paneled dining room in the main building at Pinewood Studios in leafy Buckinghamshire was always a highlight of my day, as it was a break from the trials and tribulations of the ever-escalating problems on the Monroe-Olivier set. One day, my life changed as I sat enjoying my midday break. I looked up as a truly beautiful young woman walked by my table. I thought she was one of the loveliest creatures I had ever seen. This, after six years at Paramount, was saying something. I found out her name was Lynn Tracy, and she was filming a small part in the John Gregson-starring *Miracle in Soho*. I never saw her at the studio again, but a couple of months later, at the Royal Command Film Performance, I saw her. She was one of the starlets selling programs. As I was quite busy with Monroe—the star-of-stars that night, I was not able to speak to Lynn, but I did find out her phone number from Jock MacGregor, who was in charge of the program activity.

We eventually met for dinner, but no sparks flew and I was soon to return to the States, so it was a case of "Next time I'm in London, I'll call."

When I did return but a few months later, we did meet and I invited her to come over to Paris, where I was with Bob Hope. This time there were no sparks, but rather a conflagration that only went out after forty-two years of marriage with Lynn's death from cancer of the esophagus at our home in West Sussex. A lit cigarette was as much a part of her as her ever sweet disposition.

We met in Paris or London during the rest of 1957, and I soon realized Lynn was far more suited to the world of modeling than acting. She did have one small speaking part in *Night of the Demon* (*Curse of the Demon* in the U.S.), which has become over the years a rather famous British cult horror classic. Lynn played an airline hostess with one brief "coffee, tea, or milk" line with star Dana Andrews, although her part was deleted from the U.S. release.

My wife, Lynn, in an unused scene from *There's a Girl in My Soup* for Columbia Pictures, 1970 (photograph by associate producer John Dark).

With my daughter, Kim, in Richmond, Virginia (author's collection).

After our marriage, her modeling career went from strength-to-strength in Paris, London, Rome, and New York with major couture, makeup, and perfume houses. Helena Rubinstein and Christian Dior were but two of the usual suspects.

Over the years, film locations, premieres, and festivals made for an exciting lifestyle. We lived in Paris, London, Hollywood, and New York. Our daughter Kimberley was born in 1959 in Paris. She has lived principally in Paris, London, New York, Madrid, and Florida. Tri-lingual, she lives near Seville in Andalucía and has had a successful career in alternative medicine. When younger in Florida, she bred thoroughbred race horses. A deadly tragic lightning strike left her bereft. She moved to Spain with her dog and, amazingly, with her one surviving horse, a winner named Eleven Tides (E.T.). We have become quite close and manage to get together two or three times a year.

APJAC—London
End Game

Arthur decided that there was an opportunity for APJAC to have a permanent UK office to augment the successful Hollywood/New York operation, so I was to spend some weeks in London trying to line up clients. I met with and wined and dined (when necessary) such diverse British film names as John Mills, Jack Hawkins, Ralph Richardson, George Baker, David Lean, and Anna Neagle with her producer/director husband Herbert Wilcox, plus expat Americans like "Cubby" Broccoli, Joe Newman, Charles Schneer, and Irving Allen. All were negative to the idea. I like to think that none ever became clients was primarily due to the attitude of the British and Anglicized Yanks at that time that the studio that signed them was responsible for promoting their films—and them—in the process. It was universally felt that this was an integral part of distribution charges against the film's box office income.

Broccoli made it clear that he wanted hands-on control of all publicity done on his films. His position was that he wanted to pay the salary of an employee sitting in an office "down the hall" and who was only interested in but one client—him! I was to tell many publicity offices and individuals this attitude vis-à-vis Bond marketing later on when I became his publicity director.

When I went out to the studio where Lewis Allen was directing *Another Time, Another Place*, starring Lana Turner and Glynis Johns, I wasn't introduced to the leading man—a relative "unknown" named Sean Connery. I remember hearing him speak (off camera) and thinking that, with that heavy Scottish burr, here's one actor, although very handsome, who would have a very short career. He made Corporal Fraser in *Dad's Army* sound like John Gielgud. Seven years later, he sounded as good as he looked and movie history was made.

During this period two major APJAC clients came to London (luckily not at the same time) so I became the local contact and "doer." They were Richard Widmark and Gene Kelly; I had never met either while in LA. They were both delights and the situation found me not just meeting their needs, but having occasional meals and being with them when required. I particularly remember going to a ballet with Kelly one night as a last-minute replacement for someone or other who couldn't get free. What an evening that was. This socializing with the stars was something that would never have happened back in Hollywood. Life in the upper reaches of the motion picture social divide was very pleasant indeed!

Hollywood Interlude

I returned to LA and was given a desk in Jacob's Beverly Hills office. I mention but two personalities with whom I was primarily involved back then. One was the *compère* of the successful TV show *General Electric Theater*. This host had been presenting the 20-Mule Team Borax western series for some time and the GE show was considered a step up for him in every way. His name was Ronald Reagan, and this was still a few years before his emergence as a political animal singing the praises of the conservative Arizona Senator Barry Goldwater. I spent quite a bit of time with Ronnie up at his hillside home equipped with every latest electrical innovation that GE had developed for home improvement/living. In all the time I was around him, I have no memory of his ever once expressing any thought or position that reflected a philosophical viewpoint that could be construed as political. He was strictly business but was always friendly and warm in demeanor. He never once showed a star tantrum and was no different from his Pine and Thomas days at Paramount. I'm just sorry that I never asked a photographer to take just one picture of the two of us in the same frame. I was always by the photographer's side making sure that we got pictures that might see the light of day in some publication or other! Ronnie's wife, Nancy Davis, was pleasant enough when we needed her for a "domestic" photo by a lamp or whatever.

The other name was Bob Hope. I learned he was about to start a film under his own company control to be made in Paris and to co-star the great French comic Fernandel for United Artists, so I fixed a meeting with Bob at his Valley home. The result was that APJAC was signed to handle the picture. His single proviso was that I was to be on the film in France and have no other clients to take my time and attention away from *Paris Holiday*. This was fine by Arthur and happily got me back to Europe and a certain English model/starlet whom I had left most reluctantly a few months before.

So, after a very short time, following my return to California, I was on my way back to Europe to arrange for Bob's arrival in France and to set up a publicity operation from scratch for a major production. I also had to leave an interesting personal situation—a young lady I knew ever so well was torn between two very successful young movie stars. She had known both for some time and became close to each. They were both talking "permanent" and I had become more of a confidant to her than a third "spoke of the wheel."

A well-bred, beautiful, and single woman would always be an irresistible magnet to a macho movie actor who was secure in looks and fame. A wannabe starlet is one thing, a "Dusty" Bartlett was quite a different bone-china cup of tea. Small wonder the likes of a Jeffrey Hunter was taken by the absolutely fabulous Arizona heiress that was "Dusty." They were soon to marry.

Sex Spelled Backwards
Is Pronounced Excess

People in films during the 1950s were well aware of their standing within the industry. They knew where they fit in socially. Among the "haves" if one worked at a "major," he didn't really have too much to do with those who were making films at the "minnows" unless casting on the same film brought them into temporary contact. Of course, cowboy star John Wayne got the last laugh when the former denizen of the "horseshit and sawdust" Republic Studios of Papa Yates out in the San Fernando Valley became the world's Number One Star.

The big-name actors and actresses, the top producers and directors, the studio heads, major writers and composers, and the head theatrical agency men and women of that time were the most important. Their prestige and earning power put them at the very top, a very closed society indeed. It wasn't called A-List back then, but that certainly is a perfect description.

After this *crème de la crème* were the executives, writers, directors of photography, composers, and costume and art designers, whose talents and earnings put them relatively high up on the scale, followed closely by the steady working actors (whose faces were very well known to the moviegoing public even though most would be hard pressed to come up with the right names). Then there were the studio "suits"—countless lawyers, middle management people, public relations types handling publicity and advertising, lesser theatrical agency people, and the countless technicians without whom a film could not be made. Dancers, singers, and musicians, stand-ins, extras, studio personnel (secretaries) rounded out the social interplay and all contributed to the industry ticking over.

Naturally friendship based on mutual interests made for many family get-togethers at weekends all over the Californian South Land. The point of this lesson in Filmdom Sociology is to reflect that it was primarily through good old SEX that the various levels socially interacted. It should also be noted that there were two parallel universes existing on Planet Hollywood—the hetero and the homosexual. Each flourished and the two were only united by those few whose bisexuality made them like the busy bees flitting about the flora and fauna doing their many splendored things wherever he or she found it. I had a good friend of such dual persuasion who summed it up by saying, "One gets twice as much!"

*   *   *

A very wealthy young lady from one of the oldest Los Angeles families living in Westwood was the permanent girlfriend of a very major, very aging and very married film star. I had just left her apartment and was waiting for the lift at her floor when the Hollywood hero of countless films since the dawn of talkies walked out as I stepped in. A close call! She was just another pretty face and body, but one with the money to do as she pleased ... and she certainly pleased that major star and yours truly, but her identity now is of no consequence.

Another personal involvement more fraught with danger was with a very beautiful and sensuous Polynesian-American dancer who appeared in a couple of Paramount films, which was my original connection with her. She was also very close to my best friend, a young agent I had met through our love of bullfighting. Among many others she was one of the "favorites" of a voracious Mexican-American star. One late night, someone got the timing wrong and he suddenly appeared at her door. At least I was dressed and having a one-for-the-road drink (permissible in those days) in the living room. To make an awkward story short, the hot-blooded star chased me out of the door, and I didn't stop running until I got to my car. Pedro Armendariz, another fine actor with the same south-of-the-border temper, also scared the hell out of me a few years later by flashing a pistol in his waistband on a dark street in London (yes, packing a revolver in the gun-free UK of the fifties). Would I ever learn? A famous young Italian actress stood by laughing!

A final commentary of this typical "passing parade" involved a wealthy young New York socialite. We had met at the Bel Air Hotel, where I had rented a small cabana at the hotel's pool to spend most weekend afternoons instead of at my little house in nearby Beverly Glen, a leafy, and somewhat Bohemian enclave, some thirty to forty-five minutes away from the studio to the east and the sand and surf of Santa Monica about half an hour to the west. I happily paid to have the opportunity to mix with the super-rich and super-famous who were in and out. It was all very posh and for me worth every penny from my savings. My small cabana was next to that of the famed Hollywood lawyer Greg Bautzer, a very good-looking ladies' man who later married the beautiful English actress Dana Wynter. Having known him socially never hurt my standing later on with the likes of his good friend, one Albert R. Broccoli, who was about as A-List as it was possible to get! No one ever deserved that appellation more than "Cubby."

I guess most at the hotel assumed I was from old money, even though I never made any secret of my status as a studio publicity man. Being reasonably well-spoken and with a sufficient amount of social graces, I seemed to get by. So I guess the adage "if you got it, flaunt it" applied to me at that time. How else would one be playing table tennis with a young LA socialite named R. J. Wagner before Fox felt his first name of Robert was better for a future movie star?

Anyway, I became quite friendly with Bet, who was far removed from the many "starlets" who graced the Bel Air Hotel poolside. We dated for a while and really enjoyed knowing each other's company. But one early morning "in the wee small hours" I was walking out to the parking lot as Tyrone Power pulled up in his car and walked toward the hotel. I knew where he was going and I remember thinking that I was truly mixing in very rarified company. Power even smiled and said "Hi" to someone he must have considered a like-minded *compadre*. He didn't know how right he was!

Among all the oh-so-very-many ready and very willing and able pretty women scattered in and around Los Angeles, peripatetic movie stars plied their sexual ways, and those of us who were on the fringe happily scavenged along in their wake.

Like the private relationships of the aristocracy, life in the Hollywood of the fifties and London of the sixties was like a merry-go-round; the only difference being that in film-land the horses' asses were not always made of wood.

*　*　*

I must mention two of the most sexually active and world-class star fuckers who I personally knew at this time. One was a very bright mid–European-born blonde. She was not a Gabor but was pretty enough to have been one. She worked as a teller in a Western Los Angeles branch of one of the biggest banks. There she met across her till many famous actors who would surreptitiously receive with their deposit or cash withdrawal slips her name and phone number. One cannot begin to imagine how many big movie stars she "pulled" as a result of this ploy. This anecdote alone proves the male human animal is a member of "the weaker sex" and happy to be manipulated if the result was you-know-what! Those of us plebeians in her fraternity used to call her the "Kiss and Teller Girl."

The other most prolific young lady that I knew who enjoyed sharing her many favors was a TWA stewardess based in LA who was a regular attendant in the first-class section of the Constellations that then flew back and forth between New York and Los Angeles. She was equal to anyone in her Big-Name conquests. I never inquired if she was in the "Mile High Club" but she surely was a fully paid-up member of the "Malibu Beach Sea Level Irregulars."

I can't finish this commentary on Southern California's sexual shenanigans without mentioning two sisters who were acrobatic dancers playing the clubs in and around LA I met them through my agent friend. Sadly, they weren't six foot or Swedish blonde twins (of Boy's Own sexual fantasy fame), but then one can't have everything!

In no way second to Hollywood was the scene in good old London town. My first ever stay in a hotel there was in the Dorchester, as that was the favorite of Arthur Jacobs and was our destination after my first arrival in London. I very quickly met a number of the resident expat American film community. There was a world-famous director, a few producers, two or three very successful writers (both of novels and screenplays), a couple of stars, and a smattering of distribution company executives and theatrical agency types who were all part of this 1950s London version of Hemingway's "Movable Feast" in the Paris of the twenties. The word "hedonistic" would come close to describing the way it was. Hotel suites and nearby homes and apartments became magnets for actresses, models, starlets, and wannabes who were in and out and round about our gatherings on a day-in, night-out basis (or vice versa). There were also female agents, journalists, and executives who were part of the scene, but on more or less a "strictly" business level.

As the director of publicity for Marilyn Monroe Productions, I more than qualified as a full-time member of this "Sexclusive" Club. While this poor man's version of the famed Rat Pack never achieved anywhere near the sexual success of that foursome's legendary prowess, our group did OK and I don't think anyone who was part of it, permanent or transitory, had any cause for complaint. Our Swinging London was a happy and more than fulfilling place to be, even if it was a decade ahead of time.

I got to thinking about my personal adventures in the Joy of Sex when I first came to know about the concept of Six Degrees of Separation. This later became the basis of a theory that the young actor Kevin Bacon was connected, at the time of his reaching stardom, by six interactions of his film roles with other actors to every present star in the film world. For the record, I never met Kevin Bacon, although I did come to know quite a few "hams" in my years in the movie business!

Some of the obvious ongoing and never-ending couplings that existed continued for me over the years by having a job that was just important enough to matter. This gave me the happy opportunity to interact with a fairly wide variety of members of the female persuasion and this includes a couple of stars and those now known as Hollywood wives. Oh, the joy of having been, however briefly, a "toy boy." As some wag once said, "It's better to be a has-been than a never was."

So, in connecting back or forward in time, it takes only one or two highly "active" individuals—usually a very famous actor or actress (or certainly a Howard Hughes)—to further cover a wide swath of show business humanity. By mathematical progression, I figured out that, starting with first me and the initial lady concerned (like in the famous French book/film *La Ronde*), I could by six combinations of interaction easily go back to the silent era. If one considers that sound was only twenty-seven years young in the mid-fifties, this is not really such an improbable happening in a business where sex was an acceptable part of life. The possibilities were endless and it is just as easy to project ahead with the same formula some thirty-five years and reach the millennium.

I don't observe this fact with either pride or braggadocio, but facts are facts so I am able therefore to interrelate with the names of the motion picture industry from its silent days right up to the 21st century. I'm no Kevin Bacon, but this is simply the way it was. I choose to call these phenomena my personal "Six Degrees of Fornication."

This by-the-numbers formula to connect with so many others might have extended to the world of big band music if I hadn't stupidly regressed to boyhood one night in Hollywood in the early 1950s. My apartment was but a few doors from that great young married couple better known as June Christie and Bob Cooper. She was the famous girl singer with the fabulously successful Stan Kenton Orchestra, while Cooper was its lead tenor saxophonist. As I was in the business and not married, I was asked one day by Bob if I was available to make up a dinner foursome with them and a "dear friend," another singer who was to be in LA for a two-week singing gig. I almost dropped my teeth when I went over to their flat on the evening concerned, and there sat Helen O'Connell, the truly great singer and veteran of the pre-war Jimmy Dorsey Orchestra. Her renditions of "Green Eyes" and "Tangerine" were million record sellers. In World War II, the GIs thought she was just about the cutest "girl next door" one could possibly wish to know!

I was in seventh heaven over dinner and at the club we went to for a spot of dancing. Everything went swimmingly until I made a very stupid and juvenile mistake. I more or less said that I had I first heard her and the Dorsey Band before the war and had always enjoyed her voice, beauty, and great on-stage personality. Well, it was like opening a freezer door. I had done the great no-no by alluding to the years that had passed since her real glory days and also made "fan-like" noises. Silly me!

We finally called it a night and the next day when I ran into Bob in the hall he looked at me rather pityingly and said, "Jerry, you really goofed." I'm not suggesting that if I hadn't been so naïve that anything might have happened (in my dreams!), but did I ever make sure that the question would never arise again—if you'll pardon the pun.

Two London encounters merit mention. One involved the soon-to-be infamous osteopath Dr. Steven Ward. As events proved, he got his kicks by arranging parties involving leading figures from the world of politics, show business, and society with a plethora of very pretty girls, some of whom were in it for the money while others for the fun and excitement, not to mention great food and drink. I remember meeting at his place (after their faces were spread all over the British media later on) Christine Keeler and Mandy Rice-Davies. Among the many non-pros was one very lovely girl originally from Kenya who became very much involved with both Jeffrey Selznick (David's son) and me. It later became well known that Ward enjoyed manipulating people's feelings—when not their bodies in his clinic. He certainly orchestrated the very vivacious Fay Brooke between the two of us, though we were certainly not aware of his machinations. Steven was just "doing his thing." Anyway, a few years and one husband later, our Fay married Clifford Irving, the American writer who had achieved international infamy by forging the Howard Hughes diaries.

As for Ward, Keeler, and Rice-Davies, it has been well reported how the walls (and almost the British government!) came tumbling down.

Another memory involves one very unique young British leading lady of the screen whose specialty was playing oriental music on her record player in her flat off Park Lane and sensuously performing (in costume yet!) a dance of the seven veils prior to entertaining on a more private level. A good friend of mine, an American production manager for one of the world's top film producers, was visiting London and enjoyed a date with our prima ballerina. When later we compared notes (boys will be boys), we discovered our night's entertainment was exactly the same! It was obviously a long-running West End hit, though in a private venue nearer Hyde Park than a theater on Shaftesbury Avenue. We agreed that she more than deserved what both of us felt compelled to award her—a rousing standing ovation!

*   *   *

I cannot finish this account without special mention of a couple of interesting encounters. Once I was at a lunch at Greg and Greta Peck's house up on Mulholland Drive. Some of his fellow stars at Fox were there, and when I mentioned I had to phone for a taxi to take me down to Beverly Hills, one of them offered a lift.

My "chauffeur" was one of Hollywood's best-known talents at that time, Cesar Romero, always being seen out and about with the likes of a Betty Grable or Carmen Miranda. This most likable "Latin lover" was usually described as a "perennial bachelor" in the media.

Anyway, he "made his pitch" in the most subtle and charming manner. I didn't respond and the moment quickly passed. End of story.

One of the many acquaintances made poolside at Bautzer's cabana was a delightful fellow named Walter Chrysler Junior. When he learned of our mutual Norfolk, Virginia, background, a rapport was quickly established. This led eventually to the inevitable "moment of truth."

No way did I want to make an enemy of this very nice guy with the famous name backed by all the wealth and social standing imaginable. Thinking quickly, I said, "Walter, I might try it one day and absolutely love it, but I'm just not ready yet." Thankfully, he just laughed.

I never did try it. My mistake? I guess I'll never know. The train has left the station!

Hope Is Eternal,
but Yes, Mr. DeMille

With a brief few days stopover in London to visit some friends from the previous year, I duly arrived in Paris to set up a publicity operation for the Hope production, *Paris Holiday*. I hired the unit stills photographers, Linda and James Swarbrick, with whom I first met and worked on *The Prince and the Showgirl*. I also sussed out the best special photographer knocking around Europe working on American films. This was Leo Fuchs, who became a very close friend from that time to his death half a century later. He would become a very successful film producer, separate from achieving prominence as one of the very top still photographers.

A very young American publicity man trying to make it in Europe came to my attention, and against some apprehension from the United Artists Pub/Ad honchos in New York, I hired him to work in the office as a writer. Dick Guttman went on to head one of the top PR companies in Hollywood some decades later, the Arthur Jacobs of his day, and we worked together again when he represented Pierce Brosnan. What goes around comes around.

By the time Hope was to arrive on the SS *France* in Le Havre, all was in readiness at the studio. I was very happy to meet and greet him when he docked. He was duly ensconced at the George V Hotel in Paris, and preparations continued as cast and crew arrived and assembled. Start of photography quickly followed.

One very interesting incident took place during the preparation phase. Fernandel, the French comic, spoke very little English, although he certainly was able to handle his lines as required. A script meeting was arranged at Bob's suite and "Fernny," as Bob called him, arrived. After a typical star-to-star greeting, Bob pointed to the script Fernandel was carrying and asked, "How did you like the script?" The Frenchman looked at his bilingual assistant, who quickly translated.

Fernandel then conducted what I consider to be one of the shortest but compelling script conferences ever! He picked up his copy, held a few pages together, lifted it up to show Bob—and said with great emphasis, "*Moi!*"

91

He then held up the other some ¾ of the pages and said, emphatically to Bob, "*Toi!*" (you). He then put down the script and shook his finger, as only a Frenchman can, exclaiming loud and clear, "*NON!*" That was the end of the conference, and Bob, slightly taken aback, quickly explained it was already being rewritten and that Fernandel's part was being expanded even as he spoke and not to worry. Fernandel was mollified and after a quick embrace, left. Bob quickly phoned one of his writers to get to work immediately and build up his co-

My onetime protégé Dick Guttman and his wife, Gisela. Dick is now one of Hollywood's top publicists (courtesy Dick Guttman).

star's part so there would be no more trouble. It all worked out to everyone's satisfaction, although the picture, featuring two very temperamental leading ladies, Anita Ekberg and Martha Hyer, was not too successful and joined the list of "misses" as against "hits" in the film lexicon of one Bob Hope.

French comedian Fernandel (left) mugs with Bob Hope during filming of *Paris Holiday*, UA, 1957 (UA).

The Austrian-American Gerd Oswald was the director and one of the nicest people I ever encountered in the business. He later directed (uncredited) all the German-speaking sequences for Zanuck's *The Longest Day* at the same Studio de Boulogne, where we were

The author playing a reporter in UA's 1958 Bob Hope comedy *Paris Holiday* with the lovely Anita Ekberg (UA).

filming interiors for *Paris Holiday*. One interesting sidebar to working on this film was to comment on a very pretty young English newspaper writer who came over from London to cover our film and also the set of Brando's *The Young Lions*, filming at the same time in and around Paris. It seemed to

93

be one of her first times interviewing movie stars, and her exuberant enthusiasm in her assignment to Paris and the world of international motion pictures was a delightful and charming counterpoint to the often humdrum attitudes of the usual jaded visiting press and their "what have you got for me today?" attitude. Anyway, the point of this anecdote is that this young neophyte journalist went on to become one of the most successful best-selling novelists in the world a couple of decades later. Her name: Barbara Taylor-Bradford. She is certainly one of the very successful people I have known who richly deserved fame and fortune as a result of hard work and fortitude.

Jacobs was in and out of Paris a few times during the making of the film, and on his last visit I pointedly told Arthur I was somewhat disturbed that much of my salary hadn't been deposited at my California bank. UA paid directly to APJAC the fee for all the PR services on the production, and the responsibility of passing on salaries was Arthur's. My weekly living expenses were paid at the production level, so my costs were more than covered locally. It was a matter of principal. Arthur pleaded cash flow problems in LA, as many of his clients were slow with their payments. This was one of the reasons, he then told me, that he was leaving PR and starting his own production company. He was secretly negotiating a deal with 20th Century–Fox to make a film starring a cast of almost exclusively APJAC clients like Shirley MacLaine and Dean Martin. The film was titled *Something's Got to Give*. (The film went through several iterations and ended up being Marilyn Monroe's last bit of work—the picture was unfinished.) Was I interested in staying with him in his move to production? I declined with thanks. It would have not only meant going back to the States, but the odds were great that Arthur's producer dream would end with just that one film! The big IF for me was, naturally, the odds against APJAC's success. It was one thing to be "big" in other echelons of the industry, but to have the word "Producer" before your name was another matter entirely. There have been literally thousands of men and women with the credit of producer or co-producer or associate producer or executive producer—all of whom are never heard from again! With great secrecy and promise of confidentiality, Arthur gave me an English translation of a small volume by a French novelist named Pierre Boulle. Its original title was *Planète des Singes*. He said he had taken an option on the property and, assuming all went well at Fox, he soon hoped to make a film of (in English) *Planet of the Apes*. Maybe he could cover our small financial standoff by making a gentleman's agreement (not in writing, obviously) if I agreed to receive a very (repeat "very") small percentage of any profits he might make (IF AND WHEN!!??). It was to be a verbal-only deal between us, promised in good faith as friends. I didn't have much choice, and figuring that I just had to chalk the certain loss in salary to experience, I agreed, shook Arthur's hand, and almost laughed as I thought of Pierre Boulle; had Arthur made a "monkey" out of me? A picture with talking simians! Indeed! What would Mr. Jacobs' fevered imagination think of next? However, Arthur kept his word—so I did get the last laugh and a small profit in the bargain. Dumb luck sometimes happens.

Just before *Paris Holiday* finished filming, Bob's long time personal publicist, Mack Millar, the very epitome of the highly charged New York press agent, died. It was a great loss to one and all, and I was both very surprised and flattered when offered the chance to replace him as Bob's personal publicist. I surprised both Hope and myself by refusing. It meant returning to Hollywood to live and I really wanted to stay in Europe. Also, I knew further employment was waiting for me as friends/associates at Paramount's New York head office had recently contacted me to find out if I might be interested in handling the promotional campaigns for the European releases of *The Ten Commandments* later that year. The epic was already a box office champion in the U.S. and woe betide Paramount's International Department at any lesser level of success in the foreign market place. The pub/ad hierarchy in New York knew that DeMille was vaguely aware of me from having been at the studio, so I guess they felt if he was given the chance to rubber stamp my employment in advance, if anything went wrong in Europe they were then able to say he had approved my hiring. It also didn't hurt cost-wise that I was already in Paris. If I had been in LA or New York I would never ever have been thought of. It was most expedient that I was already on the scene and known to DeMille. This is a perfect example of the film industry maxim of "covering your ass." Happily, it worked out to the satisfaction of all concerned.

Special sales and pub/ad teams were put into operation for the areas of Europe/Middle East, Far East/Australia, and South/Central America. One of Paramount's most senior sales executives, "Ricky" Michaud, was to be in charge of the European operation and be my immediate boss. A very smooth Frenchman born in Egypt, he was the personification of the cultural, urbane international mover and shaker. I truly enjoyed working in close proximity to him and he certainly smoothed out the many problems the DeMille unit faced in having to work with—but separate from—the regular Paramount European Distribution operation. It would never have worked as well as it did without Michaud at the helm.

One high spot of *The Ten Commandments* European campaign was to be a promotional trip by the great man himself to London, Paris, Bonn, and Rome. The head of the International Department at the studio was to be in charge of the trip, a delightful Italian named Luigi Luraschi. He had been hired to work in the thirties by no less a figure than the company's founder and chairman of the board, Adolph Zukor. It seems that Mr. Zukor was quite taken by the talents, lingual prowess (countless languages), and work ethic of Luraschi. The Zukors met him while they were staying in Rome, where Luigi was the concierge at the Grand Hotel. Mr. and Mrs. Zukor fell in love with his solutions to any and all problems. This great find was yet another indication of Zukor's know-how and nose for talent, be it a Mary Pickford or a Luigi Luraschi. I knew him from the studio days and we got along famously. At one time in Paris, his daughter would briefly be my secretary.

All my control of the various facets of a release campaign in more than a dozen territories had to be juggled with the plans for the arrival in Europe of Cecil B. DeMille, one of few most influential and powerful people on the planet, who was neither a royal nor a political leader. His name opened all doors and visits were easily arranged. One unforgettable time for me was in London when we went to the Hyde Park Gate home of Sir Winston Churchill. It seemed that when Churchill was at Oxford he had written an essay on Moses, and DeMille had milked this for all the publicity he could during the making of the film. Anyway, there we were, DeMille, Luraschi, me, and a couple of Churchill's people. Of the latter, one was a chap named Toby something-or-other, who was the principal functionary supervising the proceedings. DeMille (about as famous as it was possible to be) seemed genuinely moved to meet the great man and, after the introductions, said, with some (and unusual) sincerity, "Sir Winston, I can honestly say that in the whole world, yours is the hand I had most looked forward to shaking." Churchill beamed and said, "Well, shake it again!" and held out his paw. DeMille, almost tearfully, did so. Humility was not his strong suit, but I felt very moved to be present when he showed it, however briefly, in the presence of true preeminent charisma, personality, and position.

While we were in the UK the Royal Command Performance took place, and DeMille was naturally the top name in the lineup to meet the queen. The film honored was *Oklahoma!*, but *The Ten Commandments* got more than a few mentions in the British press because of DeMille's presence. In the star lineup, he did a very clever and almost unnoticed thing. When he was introduced to Her Majesty and was bowing his head as they shook hands (all normal so far), his left hand came forward and was gently placed over the queen's gloved right hand as he was shaking it. He wanted to be absolutely sure that she stayed there in front of him long enough for some good photos to be taken. What a sense of doing (in his mind) the necessary. Being an elderly gentleman helped him get away with it, plus it was done most subtly.

Almost "state visits" with President Rene Coty in France and Chancellor Konrad Adenauer in Bonn followed with much press space, and then Rome, which was to be the high point (and main reason) for his being in Europe. A papal audience had been set up as the culmination of a tie-in between Paramount and the Vatican, whereby a motion picture was to be promoted in all the Catholic churches, great and small, of an entire country. The reason was simple. The Vatican (oh-so-savvy and "with it"), had decided that a popular major film about the life of one of the Bible's most famous characters would re-energize the faith of millions who were being wooed by communism in the late fifties. I spent many days at the Papal See in its Secretariat of State setting up the details of the promotion and the forthcoming audience with DeMille and the few family members accompanying him to Rome. A couple of staff members were to be included, and I was fortunate to be one of them. I was there in tandem with Luraschi and the Italian-American monsignor who had been assigned to coordinate the Vatican's involvement with the film. When the audience ended, DeMille seemed reluctant for His Holiness to leave *his* presence, but Pope Pius had other fish to fry—if not to catch, which after all must have been part of the original "papal job description," I am sure!

A few months later, after great reviews and unbelievable box office results all over the world, I found myself in Mr. DeMille's office on the Paramount lot. He thanked me again for all my efforts, and with much emotion, wrote a comment on his favorite "fan photo" and personally handed it to me as if it were a Victoria Cross or Congressional Medal of Honor! He had pompously written "To Jerry Juroe, who has done so much to bring God's word to all people." Modesty was never my strong suit but this was way over the top! I have often pondered if that inscribed photo and five cents will get me past St. Peter.

Two footnotes—during that studio visit, DeMille asked me to be present the following week at the upcoming dinner in his honor being given by the Screen Producers Guild at the Beverly Hills Hotel. It was amazing how many of his former stars were to be gathered—a roll call of Hollywood thespians great and near-great. It really was meant as a pleasant bonus from him, so I was most pleased with the assignment. I helped organize the photo of one of the greatest gatherings of his actors from over the years, all veterans of his films. There have been other such star group photos, but that assemblage of names takes some beating. I felt privileged to be standing by the photographer helping to organize proceedings when the picture was taken. It is a history of Hollywood in one frame!

My other favorite *Ten Commandments* moment came when I had to represent DeMille and coordinate the campaign and premiere in South Africa. My English wife, Lynn, had soon before given birth to our daughter, named

Lynn and our daughter, Kim, England, early 1960s (portrait by Leo Fuchs, author's collection).

Kimberley, so it was wonderful that Lynn could come with me fully recovered and back to her beautiful model self. Our Chilean nanny took charge of our baby at the Paris apartment, so all was well. Durban, Cape Town, and Johannesburg were all an unforgettable experience and of course the smash hit success that followed was the icing on the cake. If there had been an Eleventh Commandment, it surely must have been "Thou Will Travel Forth and Promote the Picture."

Paramount—The Second Time Around

I was asked if I was available to go around the world with Paramount's vice president in charge of all foreign operations, George Weltner. The trip was to be called "Paramount's Re-affirmation of Faith in Making and Distributing Motion Pictures." I surely was available, so off we went. It was all somewhat magical to be in places like Tokyo, Bombay, Singapore, and Hong Kong for the first time and be wined and dined by the great and good of the local industry film "gods." I particularly remember a twenty-course Chinese banquet at the palatial home of zillionaire Loke Wan Tho in Singapore, where the hostess was Han Suyin, the author of the best-selling book which became a most successful film of recent times, *Love Is a Many Splendored Thing*. In Bombay, a visit to the film studio of the Warsi brothers, which soon was to become the center of what was to be known round the world as "Bollywood." I well remember going out to a Tower of Silence. This was where the upper class Parsi dead were laid out for the vultures to do their thing. Quite an experience and a rarity for a non-member of that faith to observe.

Tokyo will always be remembered for my first experience of a geisha tea ceremony in company with the most important leaders of the Japanese film industry. Traveling in company with a soon-to-be president of a major American film company is certainly to be recommended as the way to go!

Hong Kong with the Shaw brothers, Run Run and Run Me, certainly exposed one to the upper echelons of the film world, Far Eastern or anywhere else for that matter.

The offshoot of this trip for me was promotion to be full-time head of European/UK pub/ad for distribution and production.

European visits of two old friends from studio days were a welcome diversion from the everyday life of the promotion of the films that appeared like clockwork in the distribution pipeline like the little plastic white ducks at a carnival shooting gallery, one after the other. Bill Holden came over to star in *The Counterfeit Traitor*, and a pre-production trip to Berlin made for a break. It was also pleasant to meet again the famous director George Seaton

Actor William Holden strikes a heroic pose next to the infamous Moabit Prison outside Berlin for *The Counterfeit Traitor*, Paramount, 1962 (Paramount Germany).

when we met at the infamous Moabit Prison, which was to be a shooting site. Danny Kaye arrived for a European tour to promote his latest film and all went well until we arrived in West Germany. I don't know what Kaye expected, but it wasn't to find people enjoying life and totally recovered from the end of the nightmare of fifteen years before. I guess Danny still expected "sackcloth and ashes" and a people sharing a collective guilt of biblical proportions, so it really became apparent there would be a major disaster if he stayed there much longer. He was near breaking point with his barely controlled anger over all these happy and prosperous Germans. I wasn't in a position to tell him to go home, so I called Weltner in New York and explained the situation. Kaye happily accepted whatever reasons the company gave for needing him back in the States; he was gone fairly quickly.

Life in Paris was shortly followed by promotion to the top job in New York. I had to accept this post, even though I felt I might regret a move back to the States. This was somewhat allayed—again by fate—when my wife and I, traveling first class on the SS *United States*, became friends with a middle-aged couple who turned out to be extremely wealthy and socially at the top of the tree in New York. They were most interested in learning why we were on the ship and as a result almost immediately after arrival, an invitation to attend an intimate dinner at their Connecticut home with their neighbors and dear friends Mr. and Mrs. Barney Balaban was extended. Balaban was one of the most important "names" in all the world of motion pictures and was no less a figure than president of Paramount Pictures! The evening ended

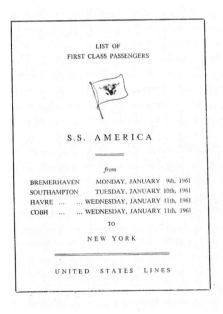

Crossing the pond: SS *America* passenger list, 1961 (author's collection).

with me being treated as his new favorite employee. It was quite something the next week when, for the first time, I went into the executive private dining room in the Paramount building for lunch with my new colleagues. There must have been six or seven VPs there, all very senior to me. Barney (he insisted I call him by his first name) made a big thing of my arrival for lunch and many a jaw dropped by one and all at the effusiveness with which he welcomed me to the New York home office. Of course, he did it on purpose; I think he enjoyed a new face around and an opportunity to stir things up a bit and then sit back to watch how it all played out over the future. That I was treated as an equal and like an old and dear friend by Balaban certainly gave me a leg-up politically, although I think a quick order to travel to acquaint myself with the South and Central American territories resulted. However, it didn't take many months for it to become obvious to me that I was not meant to be in New York, even in a coveted corner office overlooking Times Square. I longed for Mayfair, the Champs-Élysée, the Prado, and the Via Veneto!

All came to a fairly quick head when good friends at United Artists (made during the Bob Hope venture) offered me the job of director of European pub/ad for distribution and production. The prerequisite was that I advised those in charge at Paramount that it was me who initiated the contact with UA. Film companies had an unwritten agreement not to poach, although the quickest way to go upward in the corporate film world was to make a lateral move. This was tough, but I had to agree, so I asked my rich friend for another invitation to his home and to invite Barney. This was done and I, almost in tears, explained how my English wife and Paris-born daughter should live their lives in Europe where I, too, felt my future to be. Balaban said to tell my two bosses, George Weltner and Jim Perkins, that he was aware of my decision and for them to talk with him if they became "difficult." This proved unnecessary. They were true gentlemen. It also didn't hurt that I recommended that the very talented young pub/ad head for Germany should come over to take my place. He got the job and that is how a former member of the *Hitlerjugend* ended up in New York as an executive in the American film business.

All went well, but the one enemy I created by leaving was the number two in domestic pub/ad, Martin Davis, who had dreams of grandeur (which came all too true!). Though not my immediate bosses, Jerry Pickman and Davis didn't like it when someone left them. Davis' plan was to go after Weltner (who had been anointed to succeed Balaban). The arrival of Charles Bluhdorn and his Gulf and Western was still in the future, but like a master chess player, Davis was way ahead in getting to the top. Many years later, *Vanity Fair* did a major article on him, when he headed not just the Paramount subsidiary but was the chief operating officer of the giant conglomerate G+W. He was certainly no man to cross, and I was to learn this first hand when I returned yet again to Paramount in London for a third time (unlucky?) as number two of production. More later on that fractious time. Motion picture corporate politics is not for the weak-hearted.

United Artists

I moved a few blocks from my Times Square office up Seventh Avenue to the building where United Artists made its headquarters. I was to spend a couple of weeks there being indoctrinated into the UA way of doing things, getting to know most of the home office personnel with whom I would be interacting and being briefed on the people in Europe who would be my new colleagues. Almost immediately after arrival, I was thrown in the deep end of the pool and had to go to Berlin to help coordinate the gala world premiere of UA's great box office hope for the year, Stanley Kramer's *Judgment at Nuremberg*. Most of the stars would be assembled and a large gathering of the world's top cinema press would be in attendance. In my new capacity, I would be co-responsible for what was really a mini-version of a full-blown film festival—but all for just one film. My senior partner in crime in running this would be UA's number two man in Publicity and advertising, Gabe Sumner. He was roughly the same age as me and had also worked at Eagle-Lion and Paramount. Our careers were somewhat parallel, but he was further up the corporate ladder than me for sure. We made a good team and our very hard work with a large number of UA's top domestic U.S. and foreign publicity people helped make the entire event a big success. Producer-director Kramer seemed most pleased with our efforts and it provided a great introduction for me into the ranks of UA's European operation.

A few unusual happenings during this Berlin Extravaganza need mentioning. Top of the list has to be when we were told that Katharine Hepburn would be accompanying her dear "partner," Spencer Tracy, to Berlin, but that it was to be kept secret! As everybody (stars, press) would be staying at the Berlin Hilton (we had literally taken over the hotel), how were we ever to keep her presence under wraps? A late-night arrival at Templehof Aerodrome and their being spirited into the hotel's rear entrance and up to their suite in the wee small hours (when even the latest of the party-minded journalists were catching up on most needed sleep) was arranged. To my knowledge, Hepburn never once left that suite and certainly not one word of her being there ever saw print. We did all we could with payoffs to hotel employees where needed and, happily it worked.

Judy Garland arrived with a large entourage and was every inch the grande dame. I quickly made friends with her principal friend, confidante, and associate, the fabled voice coach and former singing star (in her own right) Kay Thompson. One of her earliest hit records was her song "The Steam Is on the Beam," written with Johnny Mercer. I mentioned this at the airport while greeting them, and Thompson was delighted that there was someone who even knew who she was. She was also known for a backing group in her former nightclub act named The William Brothers. She became celebrated as the discoverer of one of the younger siblings, a Williams named Andy. She also did more than all right as one of the stars of *Funny Face* as the fashion magazine editor. Her "Think Pink" number helped kick off the film and more than set the tone for that most delightful picture. She was the key to cooperation from the mercurial and oh-so difficult Miss Garland. Kay literally opened the door for our little problems and all went well, chez Judy. Kramer was amazed.

Burt Lancaster and Richard Widmark duly arrived and were most helpful and cooperative, and it didn't hurt that both were known to me from past times. Our German, Austrian, and Swiss publicity directors got full-whack out of the presence of Maximilian Schell, who was to be the only Oscar winner for his acting work on the film. We had desperately wanted Marlene Dietrich to come to Berlin, but even the several years since World War II ended was not enough time for her to agree to return to the place of her birth and initial fame. One can say what they like about her being difficult—but one has to agree that this was one lady who was absolutely true to her political convictions.

I saved mention of Montgomery Clift for last. This most troubled and off-the-wall actor's health problems and mercurial mood swings were legendary, and he needed constant attention. During the evening of the premiere, in the presence of Mayor Willy Brandt and countless dignitaries gathered at the Kongreshalle, our Monty "lost it" and—I kid you not—started crawling around on the floor. If Stanley Kramer hadn't been there immediately to take charge of a most embarrassing moment, I shudder to think what would have happened, public relations-wise. Kramer was, in my opinion, one of the friendliest and accommodating motion picture makers I ever encountered. His great creativity and celebrity was matched by his likability and understanding of how to handle the myriad of problems that are such a constant in the motion picture world, be it during production or distribution. A few years later we would do it all over again in Hollywood for the world premiere of his highly successful *It's a Mad, Mad, Mad, Mad World*, but with the accent on slapstick comedy instead of the black drama of postwar Germany.

* * *

The 1960s was a time of plenty and prosperity for United Artists in Europe but, it kept me constantly on the go. The great success of the Bond and Pink Panther franchises took up quite a bit of my time, and I was always visiting a set somewhere or other. Needless to say, the two Beatles films *A Hard Day's Night* and *Help!* made at the very height of the band's popularity were of worldwide interest. There was always a major film in pre-production and/or actually being made. To name but four, *The Train, Topkapi, Khartoum,* and *What's New, Pussycat?* were indicative of how my workload took me to many exotic places, but there seemed to be little time to enjoy my surroundings. When not on a far-flung location, I would be at some major European studio like Cinecitta in Rome, a Pinewood near London, or a UFA in Berlin.

It's the Beatles! A scene from 1964's *A Hard Day's Night* (UA/Photofest).

I will randomly cover what might be of interest as I reflect on that very busy time. It must be noted that I had to staff the publicists and photographers and oversee their work on these productions while also be responsible for the publicity and advertising of all the UA product being distributed and exhibited throughout the United Kingdom and Continental Europe. This was not an easy workload but no one could imagine a more interesting and challenging job than the one I had during most of the sixties. There is no chronological order to my listing of the films. I comment on them as they come to mind.

* * *

My first contact with producer Harry Saltzman was on his Bob Hope London–set film *The Iron Petticoat* (not UA). Bob's warm reaction to a former Paramount co-worker didn't hurt my first relationship with Harry, who must have figured if I was good enough for Bob Hope, I just might be good enough for him. My major ally in my five years of working with the mercurial Saltzman (and Broccoli) was George "Bud" Ornstein. I met him on my first trip to Spain after the Berlin premiere of *Judgment at Nuremberg*. I went to Madrid and Barcelona to coordinate the release there and encountered Bud, who was based in Barcelona and oversaw UA's European productions on the continent along with big boss Ilya Lopert, whose Paris office was just down the hall from mine.

Bud was married to a very nice lady named Gwynne, who just happened to be the adopted daughter (and blood niece) of Mary Pickford, one of the founders of United Artists along with husband Douglas Fairbanks, Charlie Chaplin, and director D.W. Griffith. Gwynne was adopted by her Aunt Mary after the very early death of her most troubled mother. As one goes through life, one meets people with whom an immediate and everlasting rapport is established and this is the way it was with Ornstein. This most likable man, who became a true friend, was shortly afterwards transferred to London and became singularly responsible for UA's name on countless hits, headed by the James Bond series, the Beatles films, and the Pink Panthers, among others.

Regarding Bond—Columbia had had the first crack at acquiring the rights. Their head of European production, Mike Frankovich, had been most interested but evidently couldn't convince his studio to finance a first Bond film. It was small potatoes money, but Bond was, after all, to be no more than a minor film with minor names. Successful in Britain, the books were not best-sellers in the States (yet) and President John F. Kennedy, being a big fan of the writer Ian Fleming, was unknown at that time. Every film company through history has had its share of mistaken turn-downs, but Columbia's rejection of Bond has to be near the top of any list of all-time filmmaking decision disasters.

Bud's enthusiasm and certainty of success ended in a meeting in New York between company president Arthur Krim with Cubby and Harry. For UA it was a seminal event of major proportion in film history, although most certainly, no one knew this at the time. Though I had met Albert R. Broccoli when I was with Monroe and later when I tried to sign him for APJAC, it was in the pre-production days leading up to the start of production of *Dr. No* that I really got to know him.

Of the countless number of people I met through the years of my working life, few had a greater influence on me than Cubby. He was the consum-

The big three: Bond author Ian Fleming flanked by producers Harry Saltzman (left) and Albert "Cubby" Broccoli, early 1960s.

mate professional as a producer and the very model of all that is admirable and honorable in the categories of husband and father. He was, quite simply, one of the finest human beings it became my distinct honor and privilege to know. I can hear Roger Moore screaming "Sycophant!" at me if he had lived to read these lines. I would tell him, Roger, I'm not trying to curry favor or guard my job—I'm just telling it like it was.

* * *

Many films were made in the studios located in the Paris suburbs to the west and east of the French capital. One of the most enjoyable to be around was *Topkapi*, directed by the American Jules Dassin and starring his wife, the very Greek Melina Mercouri. They were the very epitome of the old expression that "opposites attract." It's hard to imagine two people more different, but they were two of the happiest and contented married couples I met in all my years in movies. Fine acting combined with film directing prowess made *Never On Sunday* a worldwide hit and led to a UA deal for more films for them both. The Istanbul location for *Topkapi* was challenging, but seeing brilliant actors like Peter Ustinov and Akim Tamiroff do their thing was unforgettable. The leading male actor was the handsome Swiss Maximilian Schell. He was the very model of the perfect film hero, and what a surprise that he was a pleasure to work with. No star tantrums at all. He handled the press and photographic demands with charm and efficiency.

There is one wonderful anecdote to relate from the premiere of *Topkapi* in Athens. We all went from the theater to a famous and very large open-air restaurant to celebrate. There was a constant stream of locals and tourists coming in and winding past our table right by the dance floor. From my seat, I saw an American group come in. One of the men suddenly spotted Melina and Jules dancing right in front of him by our table. He had obviously seen *Never on Sunday* and it was more than likely that the most delightful (and successful) film had much to do with him (and his wife) being in Greece, as tourism soared due to the movie. The man stopped, his eyes popped, and he pointed excitedly at the apparition before him. It was as if he suddenly found himself in the middle of the film he had so recently seen. As our stars spun away into the dancing crowd, the wife came up to the side of her awe-struck husband to find out why he was acting like some gibbering chimpanzee. He was stutteringly trying to tell her what had happened. She was most skeptical and they were now right by my chair. I stood and told them that, yes, it was Dassin and Mercouri, and I arranged for their group to see *Topkapi* the next evening. It probably made their trip to Greece. It certainly made my night. Who needs the Acropolis when you've got Mercouri, a Greek goddess for all seasons?

* * *

Tony Richardson was a most accomplished film *auteur*, but not the easiest of people—from a publicity perspective. He really considered it beneath him and a most unpleasant sidebar to his profession as a motion picture director. Even the wildly successful *Tom Jones*, with its witty and imaginative advertising and promotional campaign, didn't change his attitude to those of us charged with the handling of his finished product. He was a regular at the European film festivals as his type of picture-making was precisely the very model of what festival honchos wanted. Tony did love the adulation and deference shown him and his films, and this made him happy. The financial success was nice if it happened, but not really that important. It was at a time in his career when he knew there was always some studio that would finance his next project, whatever it was.

He and his wife, Vanessa Redgrave, were in Paris to film their segment of *Red, White and Zero*, a three-part anthology film with different stars and directors. Unhappily, it was a bit of a bust. My most personal recollection of that production was having to go to the Richardsons' apartment off the Champs-Élysée to collect Vanessa for an interview. Her two infants were there under the watchful eye of a nanny. I made the usual sounds of approval to proud Mum as I ooh'd and ah'd over two cashmere blanket-covered little beauties. Who could guess the glamorous lives that Natasha and Joely Richardson would grow up and lead and that one would end in tragedy and an early death? As I look back on my own time on this earth, I never cease to marvel at these happenings along the way that has made mine such an eventful journey.

* * *

Paris Blues was a film made a couple of decades too soon. Its story was of a black and a white jazz musician working in a club in Paris who fall in love with two friends, one white and one black. The original idea was compelling because each romance was with a member of the opposite race. In the early sixties this would have been box-office disaster, so the obvious answer was to change the characters so it was white/white and black/black. Though not a flop, *Paris Blues* was a costly failure all the same. When the likes of Paul Newman, Sidney Poitier, Joanne Woodward, and Diahann Carroll, and a great director like Martin Ritt end up with a less than successful end-product, it is easy to realize why the motion picture business is such a risky one.

The film's special photographer, Leo Fuchs, invited me to dinner one night at Paris' great American chicken and ribs restaurant, Gaby and Haynes. The owners were a French lady and her ex-GI black husband. Leo was unique in that he never had a camera in his possession when not at work. Thus, that magic evening went photographically unrecorded to my great and lasting regret. To be sitting at a table with Duke Ellington, Louis Armstrong, and the great clarinetist Mezz Mezzrow was a once-in-a-lifetime "high." This is only equaled by my own stupidity in not having a picture taken with Ronald Reagan up at his house. Of course, he was just another actor then. For a PR man to ask for a special picture with a star was really a no-no. However, the number of pictures I have with celebrities is just a reflection—literally and figuratively—of how often I was an integral part of what was taking place and not just an observer.

* * *

Goodbye Again starred Anthony Perkins and Ingrid Bergman. I do realize it was just a movie and they were both fine actors, but a romance between the all-woman earthy Swede and the effete American college boy was just not going to work, no matter the script, the director, or whatever it takes to make a hit. That impossible pairing was only equaled by another UA dud, *Phaedra*. Even Jules Dassin and Melina Mercouri could not make a success of this update of Euripides' famous story. At least Perkins in that one played Mercouri's stepson, but no matter what the storyline called for, a T-bone steak and caramel syrup just don't go together!

* * *

When Arthur Jacobs and I were in London setting up *The Prince and the Showgirl*, we had dinner with Otto Preminger and the young Midwestern American high school girl he had chosen to play Joan of Arc. Jean Seberg was not yet sophisticated (what else for a 1950s teenager?), she was clearly out of her depth at that start of her film life. The downward slide of her career and life ended in a parked car in the Passy section of Paris some twenty years later. Hers was a mercurial existence that ran the gamut from the FBI's J. Edgar Hoover and the Black Panther movement to Jean-Luc Godard and Jean-Paul

The author (right) dining with director Otto Preminger (center) and UA's Italian publicity executive at the Venice Film Festival (UA/UIP Italy).

Belmondo (*Breathless* is a landmark film!). The acclaimed French novelist Romain Gary certainly couldn't save her. One can't but reflect, as eventful as her life was, would she have been happier if she had never left Iowa?

*   *   *

One day I was called in to Ilya Lopert's office and was introduced to the press attaché from the U.S. Embassy. It transpired that an actress, one Angie Dickinson, was coming into Paris from the location of the UA film *Jessica*, being filmed in Sicily. The order had come down from the White House that her every need was to be met while in Paris, and that publicity was to be kept to a minimum except for one controlled interview with the *Herald-Tribune*, which I was to oversee. The embassy presence was to be kept to a minimum. No problem, but to my surprise, when Angie's plane arrived, there was an embassy limousine, the chargé-d'affaires with a large bouquet of flowers and much "hoo-hawing" with a deference unusual even for a movie star. If this was the way that publicity was to be kept to a minimum, then this poor Hollywood publicist had a lot to learn from those ensconced at 1600 Pennsylvania Avenue!

Angie couldn't have been nicer and did not seem at all surprised by the "official" reception. As far as the White House was concerned, it was obvious she was doing "something" right.

* * *

I accompanied Tony Curtis on a promotional trip through Germany for the release of *Taras Bulba*. Tony was about to marry the actress Christine Kaufmann, and he was no problem in spite of his reputation for trouble due to his "extracurricular" antics wherever he was. I particularly remember going out to the set of *The Great Escape* when we were in Munich and hearing about the problems being caused by the antics of Steve McQueen and James Garner. "A couple of cowboys" was the way one of the British cast put it. My old Paramount friend and director John Sturges took it all in his stride and ended up with one of the most successful war films ever made. It was a memorable set to visit, and I later regretted that I missed by one week seeing McQueen's motorcycle jump being filmed. Oh well, win a few, lose a few.

I had to spend a few days around Frank Sinatra when he was having European showings of his company's production, *The Manchurian Candidate*. It was never easy being with him but the only upside was getting to know Laurence Harvey, an underrated actor and a truly misinterpreted man. His "fey" manner was a cover for a very sensitive and shy personality. He was forever aware of his Lithuanian roots, although he always gave the impression of being "to the manor born." His image was English upper-class, but like the Austrian born Leslie Howard, reality was something else. What you see is not always what you get.

Another surprise was meeting the French actress Delphine Seyrig. She had set the art house scene on fire with her portrayal of a woman whose past plays so heavily on her action in the present in *Last Year in Marienbad*. I had to go up to see her at her Boulogne-sur-Mer location of *Muriel*, again for director Alain Resnais. What a surprise to hear this ethereal French goddess speak perfect English—but with a Bronx New York (almost comic) accent. She had lived and worked there for years but had to return to her Paris roots to find work—and acclaim. This most beautiful of actresses was truly something else.

* * *

My first encounter with Greek director Michael Cacoyannis was when he was making *Electra*, starring Irene Papas. Along with Anna Magnani, Papas was about as formidable a woman as one can imagine. No nonsense with those two. They were feminine women to the core—but were not to be messed with or crossed. The feminist movement in the States might have been more acceptable with the input of Papas and Magnani.

The production manager for most of Cacoyannis' films was also a lady not to get on the wrong side of. She was Yael Dayan, the daughter of the famous Israeli general. Believe me, she could have been an army division commander any time she wanted. As the saying goes, "the fruit never falls far from the tree."

* * *

The set of *One, Two, Three* was as much fun to visit as the film was to see when released.

UA had a very pretty blonde working in the Munich publicity office who was the liaison with the German press for the production. Director Billy Wilder liked her around, and at the end of the filming took her to dinner as a "thank you" for her work. The next morning, Billy's writer, I.A.L. Diamond asked him how the evening went. He quickly passed around Billy's reply—"Iz, wouldn't you just know; the champagne was hot and the blonde was cold!"

Exodus was a set to stay away from, as Otto Preminger was notoriously difficult. Fortunately, he had his own PR people to meet his many demands. Okay by me. I often reflected on what it would have been like to work on a film with Preminger as director and Harry Saltzman as producer. The mind boggles!

* * *

Tom Jones is an outstanding example of the value of film editing. As good a director as Tony Richardson was, it was the contribution and innovation of his editor that helped make it an Oscar winning film.

* * *

My main memory of *Five Miles to Midnight* was accompanying director Anatole Litvak and star Tony Perkins on a promotional visit for the opening in Berlin. The earthy Litvak and the flighty Perkins were not the easiest combination to achieve publicity—but we all did our best. The film deserved to flop.

* * *

I spent a lot of time out at Paris' Studio Boulogne for Billy Wilder's production of *Irma La Douce*. A marvelous example of set design, plus Shirley MacLaine and Jack Lemmon did their best, but somehow or other the film never was as good a "meal," as its strong ingredients should have made it. It certainly never achieved the success of *The Apartment*, although all concerned deserved an A for effort.

* * *

Our small budget British and Irish films kept me on planes to Dublin and London with great regularity. I was always amazed at how plain and introverted Rita Tushingham was in person but how delightful she was in her various screen personae. I guess it's what they call acting.

I always liked Larry Harvey, but his first directional effort on *The Ceremony* was really a very sad result for all concerned. The directorial debuts of most actors (Marlon Brando, Roddy McDowall, etc.) show a degree of pretentiousness that is really quite astonishing.

* * *

I have read more scripts than some people have had hot dinners, but the one I remember as a comedic gem was *What's New, Pussycat?*, the first screenplay by the New York stand-up comic Woody Allen. I was sitting at the Doney Café on the Via Veneto in Rome and I was literally laughing out loud as I first read it. A very rare occurrence. It was really funny in situations and in dialogue. I was so impressed that I phoned fabled producer Charles Feldman in London to tell him that I felt UA was sitting on a major film hit. Charlie was really pleased by my call. I was really just a minor executive, but I guess he liked my chutzpa, a very favored word at the company that was United Artists.

Feldman had run one of the most successful theatrical agencies in Hollywood and had morphed from that into a dealmaker extraordinaire. He was financially into some of the most profitable box office hits of the fifties and also first discovered the talents of a young agent in LA named Albert R. "Cubby" Broccoli. Charlie had also acquired the rights to make *Casino Royale*, the first Ian Fleming novel, but none of the other Bond stories, as they weren't available.

I had not known Feldman for long but, for some reason known only to him, he accepted my thoughts, reactions, and opinions almost as an equal. Without realizing it, I became his "inside man" in his interaction with United

Artists. Not in any financial sense or as any kind of dealmaker, just a source as someone aware of how the wind was blowing. I was flattered by his attention and was happy to be acknowledged by him.

What's New, Pussycat? was originally to be filmed in Rome, but there was a never-explained problem with either Peter O'Toole or Peter Sellers that meant the whole production was moved to Paris. Despite the countless changes in the script, due to the two Peters' never-ending complaints, the film got made and Woody Allen saw his role diminished from almost equal importance to that of a lesser character on the periphery of the action. Small wonder he took control of the rest of his glittering career. The leading ladies all had their problems. Ursula Andress still represented a relatively small talent with an admittedly beautiful body topped by an equally lovely face. Paula Prentiss was a bundle of nerves and paranoia who became so out of it that at one point her actor/director husband, Richard Benjamin, had to fly over from California to settle her down to the degree that she could finish the picture. Capucine, that most mysterious of actresses (and much rumored inamorata of Feldman) always had the same expression and tone of voice, no matter the scene. She was "there," but one was never really sure. A lovely person away from filming, but in a scene on the set she never seemed to be of this earth. Finally, there was Germany's famed "Sissi," Romy Schneider, in the principal female role. Suffice it to say she was known to many of the crew (for her officious and superior manner) as the "Nazi Shirley Temple," making that one of the great oxymorons of all time.

One day a few months after the completion of the film, my phone rang and it was Charlie calling from Hollywood. He said, "Jerry, I want to know what you think of our title song?" I then heard him say "Play it, Burt!" and I sat and listened over the phone to famed composer Burt Bacharach sing while playing. Talk about a personal command performance! While I was most sincerely effusive in my reaction to Feldman, little did I realize I was one of the first people on the planet to hear the words and music of what became one of Tom Jones' greatest hits. Both song and film of *What's New, Pussycat?* were runaway financial successes and I was most happy with my small contribution.

I later learned that Feldman made no secret of his pleasure with my efforts to the powers that be back in New York. No raise in salary naturally (it was UA after all), but it was nice to be appreciated.

One sidebar to this film is to remark that once during filming, when I was invited by O'Toole to join some of his cronies in a night on the Paris tiles with his good friend Richard Burton, who had filmed a walk-on bit that day in the famed Crazy Horse Saloon, one of the principal locations. When we all broke up, back at the Plaza Athénée all the worse for wear, Peter gave me a very boozy goodnight kiss right on the lips. There was nothing sexual in it, just a very drunk Irish thespian thank you for being one of his companions on a really fun night.

* * *

Melville Shavelson had been one of Bob Hope's most successful early writers and went on to a very good career (with partner Jack Rose) as film-makers at Paramount. I got to know him fairly well during my sojourn at the studio, so I was very pleased when his next film was announced with production in Israel. This star-studded story of Israel's fight for independence was titled *Cast a Giant Shadow*, and was the story of West Point graduate Mickey Marcus who, after resigning his U.S. Army commission, ended up the first general of an Israeli army since Joshua. A large contingent of U.S.

and international press was organized to visit the Tel Aviv location to not only meet and interview Kirk Douglas, Yul Brynner, and Senta Berger, but also John Wayne and Frank Sinatra, who had small but colorful cameos. I also met for the first time the young Israeli actor Chaim Topol, whose specialty was playing very old men. He literally transformed himself in the most amazing fashion. Later he was a wonderful Tevye in UA's *Fiddler on the Roof*. The press visit was also coincidental with the anniversary of Marcus' death (shot accidentally by an Israeli patrol

With Yul Brenner (left) at the Berlin premiere of *The Ten Commandments*.

on the eve of the 1948 victory). Shavelson wrote a very amusing book on his experiences titled *How to Make a Jewish Movie*. It was more successful than the film. At distribution time we called it *Cast a Giant Turkey*.

* * *

The old RAF airfield north of London where *633 Squadron* was filmed was a most enjoyable set to visit for me and I thought Cliff Robertson portrayed a most believable Canadian pilot. The most notable element to the film was the stirring title music, a martial gem by Ron Goodwin, which is played by the RAF band to this day. Other than that notable exception, the picture went down in flames.

* * *

My contribution to the second Beatles film came about on a delightful visit to the Austrian ski resort of Obertauern, where the location filming

An original quad poster for *Help!*, featuring my idea: the Fab Four making the title in flag semaphore (UA/Photofest).

took place. I arranged for the Fab Four to be photographed on a snow-clad mountainside holding their arms in the shape of the semaphore spelling of H-E-L-P. I thought nothing more of it until I saw New York's advertising campaign months later. There was my "directed" photos of each with arms outstretched, at the top of the main poster ad art. They were always cooperative as far as I was concerned, but I never felt one ever really knew them, even when we were all together in Salzburg promoting the premiere release and in the same hotel for hours. Paul was the key to getting things done. John thought a while and eventually agreed, while George and Ringo would always agree if the other two felt whatever had to be done was worthwhile.

* * *

What can one say about Peter Sellers? He was without a doubt a comedic genius, but the word "flawed" must have been coined with him in mind. He was mercurial to a degree that beggared belief. He also had an inferiority complex which was kept well-hidden by an extrovert, almost manic manner. He constantly needed reassuring that he was the Greatest, the Muhammad Ali of humor. He also never met a beautiful woman he didn't covet, and if the attraction wasn't returned in spades he sulked in self-doubt for days on end. His likes and dislikes were immediate and all the reasoning in the world fell on deaf ears if one had the nerve to dare tell him of the error of his ways. I had to replace publicity/photographic people on three separate occasions during the Pink Panther series because of his antics.

I have two main memories of my time around Sellers. One was in his suite at the hotel Le Meurice in Paris, when he "acted" out the entire script for his upcoming production *After the Fox*. I sat alone watching a command performance with the performer doing the commanding. Those thirty to forty minutes were awe-inspiring, but very scary at the same time. He was almost deranged in his desire to prove to a UA executive, albeit a very minor one, how great his new production was going to be. He knew I was but a phone call away from the main honchos in New York. I felt like screaming, "Peter, the budget has already been approved, everything is all set. You don't have to sell it to UA anymore." Of course, I had to sit there, very uneasy at being one-on-one with this crazy actor while laughing and making all the right positive commentary until he finally announced, "The End." When I finally got down to the lobby, I went straight to the bar for a quick one. I had to mentally make my way out of Bedlam.

The other Sellers happening also took place when he and his dear friends

My wife, Lynn (in back), with Bond girl Zena Marshall and Peter Sellers during the San Sebastian Film Festival, 1950s.

director Bryan Forbes and actress wife Nanette Newman were over in Paris for a couple of days relaxation after working on a non–UA production in the UK. They were visiting our penthouse apartment close to the Seine with a balcony affording a very close view of the nearby Eiffel Tower. If one was to be an American in Paris, then milk it, baby, milk it!

It was a Sunday morning in August and there was a happy gathering over coffee and croissants, when the door to the kitchen was half-opened and the husband of our maid motioned to me rather urgently. I went in to him and he showed me one of the big Sunday papers headlining the news of Marilyn Monroe's death in California. I returned to the living room ashen-faced, and when asked what was wrong, I showed everyone the paper and its big black headline. Peter became hysterical and, without a word, ran out of the apartment.

A very frantic two days later he finally showed up at his hotel. What I didn't know was that he had secretly signed to co-star with Monroe and Frank

Sinatra in *Kiss Me, Stupid* for Billy Wilder. It could have been the second coming of *Some Like it Hot* and Sellers saw it all go out the window. Monroe's death was beyond his obsessive control of life and career. All of us, including many various UA execs, went through a crazy couple of days as a result of Sellers' disappearance. Not one word of the affair was ever picked up by the press. As the old saying goes, "all's well that ends well!"

As for the film, it did get made, but with Kim Novak, Dean Martin, and Broadway's Ray Walston in for a no longer interested Sellers. The original cast might have made the brash "near-the-knuckle" sexual content work, but it never reached the original promise. Years later, talking about the picture, Wilder wryly said, "Maybe if I had made the title's middle word IT instead of ME, I might have had a hit!"

*   *   *

I was at an Athens studio meeting with the production publicity team just in advance of the start of *Zorba the Greek.* The morning of my second day there was a call from Ilya Lopert in Paris. He told me to leave the meeting, go to my hotel, and immediately call him back. I did as directed and was told to leave for Paris on the next available flight. It seemed that Arnold Picker, UA's senior VP, learned that Michael Cacoyannis had budgeted separate fees for himself as producer, director and co-writer. Picker was outraged. Cacoyannis had not done anything really wrong, but Arnold felt that our Greek filmmaker was trying to take advantage of the company. The offshoot was that UA immediately announced that it was dropping the picture. Within two days, *Zorba* was picked up by Fox and became a really big worldwide hit.

A couple of years later, I was at the Venice Film Festival with Picker and asked him, almost like a student would ask a professor in a college tutorial, "In view of the major box office and critical success of *Zorba*, did he regret canceling the production for UA?" He answered with great feeling, "I would do it a dozen times over. Michael was trying to take advantage of UA and I just can't accept that kind of behavior by one of our filmmakers." I guess that the accountants at 20th Century–Fox reflected happily on UA's intransigence. Personally, one had to admire Arnold Picker's commitment to what he sincerely felt to be in the best interests of his company. He was a great executive without a doubt, although he was very stubborn once he decided on something, right or wrong.

Arnold Picker was one of the distribution greats and really ran the day-to-day life of UA. Arnold's brother Eugene ("Gene") specialized in exhibition.

Gene's son David Picker was to become pre-eminent as a production executive. Along with Bud Ornstein in London, David deserves a lion's share of the credit for the fifty-plus years that UA's name is on the Golden Goose that is the James Bond franchise. The world of film changed in the sixties, and David Picker was the right man in the right place at the right time!

* * *

There are many memories of countless film festivals for UA pictures, but there are a few incidents that stand out. Star Anne Bancroft and director Arthur Penn came to the San Sebastian Film Festival for the first European showing of *The Miracle Worker*. Their professionalism was exemplary and it was, as always for me, refreshing when major "names" were so cooperative. Her Oscar for Best Actress was very well deserved.

Peter Sellers came to the same festival that year to promote his latest UA release and, happily, was on his best behavior. It was all most productive, publicity-wise.

At Cannes, a small British film titled *The Knack* was to be shown in competition. Michael Crawford, later to find major fame as the title character in *Phantom of the Opera* in the West End of London and on Broadway, was the star turn in attendance. A very attractive young British woman showed up one day and announced to us in the publicity office at the Carlton Hotel that she had been in a couple of scenes in the waterskiing sequence. She was in Cannes with her parents and sister and might there be tickets? Suddenly having a very photogenic "actress" available for the voracious Cannes photographers was a big plus so, most definitely, tickets were available; but might we ask for her cooperation by doing some publicity? That was the start of her career in France. She was very lovely, but her slightly older sister was the real knockout in that family in my mind. This sister was to die tragically just a couple of years later. As for our ingénue, thrown in at the deep end of promotion at a major film festival, she did more than all right for herself in the later years by becoming one of the most famous non–Gallic movie stars of France's long cinematic history. Her name—Charlotte Rampling.

There were many filmmakers who were the scourge of people in the publicity field. One of the most infamous in this regard was the ever-so-Teutonic director Otto Preminger. One night at a beautiful dinner at the Venice Festival, Otto said, "Jerry, I find it very rare to get along with someone in your field. Why is this?" I answered that amazingly I never actually was on the set of any of his productions, not even *Exodus* in Israel, so, out-of-sight, out-of-mind. Otto gave a big smile and said, "Ah, that explains why I like you."

My principal memory of Sicily's Taormina Film Fest was of the beautiful hotel on the cliff with Mount Etna's volcano in the distance, and that other very volatile and unpredictable force of nature, Tony Curtis. This world-class womanizer was unequaled at living in the fast lane. While always friendly and cooperative, his actions put the fear of media scandal always there for those of us whose *raison d'être* was to just "sell" a film.

We promoted with great regularity each new Bond film with countless billboards up and down Cannes' Promenade de la Croisette. The front of the flagship Carlton Hotel was always ablaze with images of Connery and successors. Harry Saltzman was a great Francophile and never failed to be at Cannes. One year there was a ticket problem for a must-see major film. That he didn't get A-class tickets was no fault of mine—but I was the face of United Artists as far as Harry was concerned and it was my entire personal fault. He became so irate that I left his suite. That evening I phoned Arnold Picker in New York, said I was going back to Paris, and that he had better get someone or other quickly down to Cannes to take my place. It was a calculated risk that might have got me fired, but I was that upset. Arnold told me to settle down, stay in Cannes doing my job, and leave Harry to him. I don't know what he said to Saltzman, but the next morning there was a knock on my door at the Carlton and a dozen beautiful Baccarat roses in a crystal vase were delivered with a handwritten card. It simply said, "Jerry—even when I hate UA, I love you…. Harry." When we later ran into each other in the lobby, we fell in each other's arms. A real "luvvy" moment.

The first public showing of *A Man and a Woman* at Cannes was my most memorable film festival experience. It was a night of magic and the international audience just went nuts over the picture. UA had picked up the movie for world distribution (outside France and the French speaking territories). It was a great coup for Lopert, and I enjoyed kudos as a result of my enthusiasm and support for the film from Day One with my pub/ad colleagues in the home office. UA broke even on its purchase from the music and LP sales alone, so the box office receipts were all gravy! A winner for all concerned, especially director Claude Lelouch, as he made his pile on UA's *Vivre Pour Vivre* as a direct result of the earlier success.

Some random observations from a couple of Venice Festivals. One was seeing a young Julie Christie totally ignored—this just before her fame in

Darling. She was not yet the beauty she became in countless films in years to come; no, she was not even photographic fodder. Paul Newman was brought in to promote a film. He was most petulant and really wanted to be anywhere but by a not very sleepy lagoon. Years later in New Haven, Connecticut, for the premiere of Universal's *Slap Shot*, he was delightful and very cooperative. I guess in Venice he couldn't get his necessary supply of cold American beer, which he seemed to crave the way some people desire to find air to breathe. His intake of the brew was never ending. Amazingly, it never affected him one jot.

After the finish of filming of *The Train*, I had to accompany Burt Lancaster on a PR visit to Italy. This is memorable only to record one happening. We were leaving the Excelsior Lido Hotel to take the motor launch over to the city for a festival press activity and were walking along the hotel's dock when an incoming "vaporetto" deposited Arnold Picker and other UA execs just in from the airport. Lancaster saw them in the near distance and under

The author (left) making a point to Ed Sullivan (center) and Burt Lancaster on the set of *The Train*, 1964 (UA).

his breath almost spat out, with all the venom and menace a master actor can generate, one word—"Accountants!" So much for biting the hand that feeds you.

The Train was a really big budget production, and UA treated it with all the attention that all the money being poured into the film demanded. Any film with Burt Lancaster would always have its problems, and *The Train* had its share, primarily the replacement of director Arthur Penn with John Frankenheimer a couple of weeks into the filming. The great British actor Paul Scofield and the equally magnificent French actress Jeanne Moreau could never quite make the film reach its original promise. Even a highly promoted head-on collision between two trains proved of little consequence. A couple of heads rolled at UA, and I would have been one of them except for publicity VP Fred Goldberg's timely intervention on my behalf. I had become too close to the production and that sometimes was not a good thing.

* * *

Stanley Kramer's follow-up to *Nuremberg* was the farce comedy crime caper, *It's a Mad, Mad, Mad, Mad World.* Just about every famous comic available was in the picture and no less a star than Spencer Tracy played the chief of police in the small Southern California town who ends up with the loot that the various comedians had spent some two hours "madly" trying to find. One of the largest international gatherings of show business journalists ever were flown to Los Angeles for the premiere with UA's publicity people in attendance. There would be two days for interviews, photos, and what-have-you. One could have made a very nice little movie with the cost of that premiere trip for the European contingent alone.

I'll never forget the meeting of the cast at Stanley's palatial home in the Hollywood hills before we all left by bus for the cinema and a sumptuous gala dinner. All the comics were gathered in a room at Stanley's house before we left, which meant the inevitable "I'm funnier than you" contest. The winner without a doubt was Jonathan Winters, although a couple of months later, when I was with Milton Berle in Germany, I reminded him of the night and how I thought *he* was the Top Gun of that incredible assemblage of funny people. In my life of working with the stars, I had to butter up more egos than most people had to put on their breakfast toast.

* * *

Comedians were also much in evidence in Madrid when *A Funny Thing Happened on the Way to the Forum* was made. Producer Mel Frank (another Paramount and Bob Hope alumnus) and director Richard Lester gathered a stellar list for this filming of the Broadway stage hit. It was to star Zero Mostel, along with comics of the standing of Buster Keaton and Phil Silvers (one of the funniest of the *Mad World* cast). The young male lead was Michael Crawford, whose one "light" song gave no indication of his Broadway singing fame still a few years in the distance.

* * *

Khartoum was probably conceived to have the potential of a *Lawrence of Arabia*, but General "Chinese" Gordon was no T.E. Lawrence, and unfortunately the laid-back character of Gordon as portrayed by Charlton Heston was not quite the charismatic desert prince played by Peter O'Toole. A small bank of the Nile setting just south of Cairo made for a unique location, and that fabled city was not usually on my rounds of exotic locations. Dinners with Chuck Heston were always most pleasant.

I caught up with Larry Olivier back at Pinewood Studios during his interior scenes and he was as charming as ever. I thought, however, his playing of the brown-skinned Mahdi owed more to a slightly lisping Othello than Saladin. All that was missing was a Desdemona. However, female characters were thin on the ground in the script of *Khartoum*. Box office success was also not much in evidence sadly.

One day Bud Ornstein called me to his office to advise that the company had just picked up a film already in production at Pinewood—would I look in on the set and make myself known to director Peter Brook? It was titled *Marat/Sade*, and the players were the Royal Shakespeare Company's original stage cast. On my return to the office, Bud asked what I thought. I responded that what with the low pick-up price, UA would probably see a profit, but not to expect any publicity value from any of that cast, about as unattractive a bunch of thespians as can be imagined. A couple of years later, Glenda Jackson became living proof why I was not a casting director.

* * *

The Honey Pot was a re-working of *Volpone* and Venice's Opera House was an awe-inspiring setting but producer/director Joe Mankiewicz was no longer the creative force of his *All About Eve* days. Rex Harrison was his usual

The author (center) with three Oscar winners: filmmaker Joe Mankiewicz (left), star Rex Harrison (right front) and actor Cliff Robertson (partially obscured) on the set of *The Honeypot*, UA, 1967.

impossible self and his then-wife, Rachel Roberts, did all she could to match his "charm." At least she wasn't in the cast! At the end of filming, UA would have saved hundreds of thousands of distribution dollars if Joe had accidentally dropped the negative in the nearest canal.

* * *

The Bavarian castle location for *Chitty Chitty Bang Bang* was as magical as the Disney World logo it inspired, but those of us at UA thought the musical was a rather weak attempt at trying to emulate the box office success of *Mary Poppins*. How wrong time has proved us to be. It is now a worldwide classic of the musical stage and is yet another example of the Broccoli family show business acumen.

* * *

All the many film successes of Tony Richardson led to the company agreeing to a really big cast with a budget to match in an extravaganza titled *Charge of the Light Brigade*. Of interest is that when UA pulled the plug on any more investment in the highly over-budget "epic," Tony had whole bridging sequences animated to save money. Some film critics hailed this as innovative directorial technique—shades of *Tom Jones* to those of us in the know. On the night of the premiere, I spoke by phone with one of my bosses in New York. When he asked me how it went, I just couldn't resist my usual smart-ass attitude and merely said, "Into the Valley of Death Rode United Artists."

*   *   *

The sales head in Italy was a very warm and sympathetic man who was the antithesis of the hard-nosed American New York businessman. His name was Lee Kamern and it is necessary to mention his mother in relation to these comments. In her youth, she was the premiere piano player in the nickelodeons around New York, where she did the accompaniment to the silent action up on the screen. She was a force in the early days of the Musician's Union and knew every important East Coast musical figure. This background is the connection that one day in Rome found me to be at a lunch Lee gave for one of the greatest names in America's big band history, the famous clarinetist Artie Shaw. He was certainly one of the most intellectual and erudite characters I have ever met. I mention this only to salute this man who was as famous for his marriages (Lana Turner, Evelyn Keyes, and the daughter of Jerome Kern among others) as his musicianship.

No matter the subject, he knew it in depth and expounded on it with a clarity and insight that was little short of amazing. I'm sure he would have held his own in the presence of Einstein, as I'm equally certain that Albert would never have even known the melody of "Begin the Beguine."

*   *   *

We had a London premiere of Judy Garland's film *I Could Go on Singing*. Her then "guru," David Begelman (later the ill-fated head of Colombia Pictures), took full advantage of my help in controlling Miss G. I'll long remember our problems when she sat in the wrong seats at the cinema and wouldn't budge in spite of all the protestations. Even her co-star and dear friend Dirk Bogarde was loathe to cross her that night. We had invited at least one star from each of the main European countries to attend, and from Italy came its

A spot of bother: Actor Dirk Bogarde (second from right), Judy Garland's agent David Begelman (center, later the ill-fated Columbia Pictures president) and I (left) try to get a *very* reluctant Judy to move seats at the London premiere of *I Could Go on Singing*, UA, 1963.

famous actor, Raf Vallone. In the Savoy Hotel the day of the interviews, an elderly concierge calmly announced over the intercom, "Call for Mr. R-A-F Vallone, call for Mister R-A-F Vallone."

United Artists' James Bond

Over the years of my tenure with UA in Europe, the first five James Bond films were made, so I was in on this phenomenon from Day One. I remember being called over to the South Audley Street offices of EON Productions to be introduced to Sean Connery. I recalled as I walked up the few steps to EON's entrance in the heart of Mayfair the agonizing time the two producers and UA's Ornstein had gone through with the home office in the search for a star to play Ian Fleming's very macho gentleman spy. Countless names (mostly American!) and many weeks went by but, for once, it all worked out. It should be noted that Broccoli's wife, Dana, was one of the principal champions for Connery to get the part. Her immense and continuous contribution behind the scenes to the success of the series eventually became known and properly recognized.

The oh-so-steady and always in control Broccoli was a perfect match for Saltzman, who could be dazzlingly brilliant with his wild ideas and ingenuity. They really were a potent pair and played UA to a standstill with what was to be one of the truly great "good cop/bad cop" partnerships. As the series (and profits) got bigger, their demands on my time grew accordingly—but nothing breeds success like success. Never before had there been print and TV media around the world pleading to be given material about James Bond and his cornucopia of lovely ladies. Because EON had its own in-house production publicity team with good people in the jobs, my direct concern

And so it begins: The author (far left) sitting at a gaming table with a young Sean Connery (center), casino staff and two of the "matched set" women (the redhead, front, and the brunette, back) in the Italian Alps on the *Dr. No* press tour, 1962 (author's collection; *Dr. No* © 1962 Danjaq, LLC, and Metro-Goldwyn-Mayer Studios Inc. All Rights Reserved).

during the production of *Dr. No* was always minimal, but I still spent time on the sets at Pinewood—not Jamaica, alas—and in my constant meetings with Cubby and Harry in their office. This latter personal involvement with our two soon-to-be-moguls grew with the passing of the years and the crazy ever-rising grosses in profits. By the time I left UA, I found myself spending more time with EON than in my own office in the heart of deepest Wardour Street, most certainly a less salubrious environment than the well-kept streets and buildings of Mayfair's West One.

I got along with Connery, and all the later personal problems between Sean and EON involved UA to the degree that they wanted to keep him as 007. I liked Sean, but one certainly had to watch oneself with the mercurial Scot. Years of experience in dealing with people like Bogart and Brando paid off in that regard!

It fell to me to take Connery on his very first promotional tour (to Italy) and I came up with the idea of a blonde, brunette, and redhead to travel with him—"Bond was always accompanied by a matched set." While we were in Milan, a journalist first came up with the expression—in English—to call Bond "Mister Kiss Kiss Bang Bang." That descriptive went around the world; later a film was made with that title and no less a figure than Pauline Kael of the *New York Times* adopted it for a book title. It was fixed for Connery and the women to go up to one of the giant gambling complexes between Genoa and Bologna in the Italian Alps. UA's Italian PR people prearranged for this unknown actor playing James Bond to break the bank for real at a major European casino. It all went well with very shady looking Italian "gentlemen" watching over our every move. The story went out on the wires and, most importantly, broke in the U.S. press and even made the pages of one of New York's top tabloids.

This didn't hurt one bit the hastily arranged re-release of *Dr. No* in America. UA Sales originally mishandled (they knew not what they had) the first openings to the degree of showing the film in drive-in theaters in the U.S. South and Southwest. Not even the New York art cinema crowds were considered to be an audience appreciative of Mister Fleming's subject matter. Thanks to the very good results in Europe, a rare second full release was scheduled for the States, and this resulted in enough success to assure the company financing a second Bond film. A near distribution failure was turned into one of the longest lasting and most financially successful movie franchises ever. Fifty years and counting!

From Russia with Love was really the film that cemented the immediate future of the Bond brand. An excellent plot with a great title, it also had two of the better Bond villains in the persons of Lotte Lenya and Robert Shaw. Lenya was famous enough to have her name in the lyrics of "Mack the Knife," as she was one of the great stars of pre-war German show business as well as being the wife of composer Kurt Weill, Germany's answer to Cole Porter and Irving Berlin combined. Her playing of the Russian colonel with a hint of lesbian interest in the character of Tatiana Romanova was years ahead of its time.

Shaw was a fine British stage actor, sort of a road company Richard Burton (not bad at all!) years away from the worldwide fame he would achieve playing the fisherman of the largest and meanest man-eating shark ever to terrorize cinema audiences from Aruba to Zanzibar. The cast was rounded out with Pedro Armendariz (Mexico's most renowned motion picture actor) and the lovely Italian actress Daniela Bianchi, who played Romanova. While very pretty, hers was the only element that was not a vast improvement over *Dr. No*. After all, with apologies to Miss Bianchi, who could really follow the sexual beauty of Ursula Andress? While Bianchi never became a big film star in Italy after Bond, her voice *was* heard by countless millions as the announcer of times and flights for the Italian National Airline, Alitalia, at its various airports. It is of interest that the steamy scene where Bond first encounters Tatiana naked in bed in his Istanbul hotel room became the future screen test setting used for countless and seemingly never-ending Bond "wanabees" in the years to come when so many diverse actors were considered whenever Connery or Moore were no longer looming large as the lead in the next Fleming title on the 007 treadmill.

Goldfinger made an international star of the German actor Gert Frobe, even though his guttural accent meant redubbing for the final version. No matter the voice, the iconic line, after Bond asks if Goldfinger expects him to talk, replies, "No, Mr. Bond, I expect you to die!"—is one of my personal two or three all-time favorite pieces of dialogue from all the 007 films.

Hawaiian-born Harold Sakata, who played Oddjob, was the personification of the term Gentle Giant. His lack of English didn't matter, as his character was all action, no words. This brings to mind one of the very best Bond trivia questions of them all: What is the connection between Sir Winston Churchill and the Bond movies? The answer: The flat top high black bowler as worn by Churchill throughout World War II is the exact same style as the one chosen to be worn and used as a weapon by Oddjob!

The Aston-Martin DB5 was of minor interest during filming as no one

A curious gendarme inspects Bond's DB-5 during the *Goldfinger* Paris premiere, 1964 (courtesy Dave Worrall/Cinema Retro, *Goldfinger* © 1964 Danjaq, LLC, and Metro-Goldwyn-Mayer Studios Inc. All Rights Reserved).

then was aware how large these cars would loom in the history of the Bond franchise. We quickly found out!

What we in publicity did become aware of was the great interest of the international press in the phenomenon that James Bond had become. In the U.S., the desire of journalists to visit the location at the Miami Fontainebleau Hotel was overwhelming, and the masterstroke of Ian Fleming's name of the leading lady, Pussy Galore, caused a furor that helped seal the day for a wild press interest in the Bond films.

Thunderball was for me its female lead. I adored Claudine Auger. She was one of the most cooperative and friendly of all the Bond leading ladies. Maryam d'Abo of *The Living Daylights* was her equal in charm, warmth, and cooperation, as was Maud Adams (*The Man with the Golden Gun* and *Octopussy*). They will always rate high for me. I did not react favorably toward *Golden Gun*'s Britt Ekland and I know I was not her favorite person on the set either. It does take two to tango I guess. Lois Chiles' moods were mercurial.

There was an interesting happening post-production in Paris during a publicity photo shoot with Claudine Auger—I don't remember the name of the American photographer, but I do recall that day he had a ping pong table in a corner of his spacious studio. He knew I played, and the morning of the session he said a friend of his from the States was in town and would be there soon and might want a game. One of the tallest men I had ever seen soon walked in the doorway. We had a couple of spirited games with a split at one win each. We were about to play the deciding game but Claudine's arrival finished our contest. I didn't really pick up on who my very serious and competitive opponent was until later as he was never introduced. I guess it was assumed by our mutual photographer friend that I would know Wilt Chamberlain when I saw him!

UA had a major gathering of its international sales and PR people in London in coordination with the filming of *You Only Live Twice*. Everything that constituted the Pinewood back lot was taken up with the volcano set, and it remains one of the most spectacular for me personally. Broccoli

Claudine Augier in a publicity pose for *Thunderball*, on location in the Bahamas, 1965 (*Thunderball* © 1965 Danjaq, LLC, and Metro-Goldwyn-Mayer Studios Inc. All Rights Reserved).

and Pinewood's combined plan for a really giant stage (the 007 Stage, as it would be named) to be built came about as a direct result of problems with filming space for *You Only Live Twice*.

During those first five Bond films, I never visited a location outside of Europe, but I would have liked to have been in Japan when the car was dropped from the helicopter into Tokyo Bay. Oh well, beggars can't be choosers!

Under the volcano: UA's international executive team on Ken Adam's magnificent volcano set for *You Only Live Twice*, Pinewood, 1966. I'm in the middle laughing at a comment from publicity executive Tom Carlyle (behind me), UA vice president Fred Goldberg is next to me (glasses) (*You Only Live Twice* © 1967 Danjaq, LLC, and Metro-Goldwyn-Mayer Studios Inc. All Rights Reserved).

At left, with lovely Japanese star Mie Hama on a lunch break from filming *You Only Live Twice*, with Harry Saltzman, actress Karin Dor, Cubby Broccoli, star Akiko Wakabayashi, Ken Adam, UA exec Ashley Boone and Italian and German UA publicity executives, Pinewood, 1967 (*You Only Live Twice* © 1967 Danjaq, LLC, and Metro-Goldwyn-Mayer Studios Inc. All Rights Reserved).

My everlasting major memory of those early films was in Paris for the premiere of *Goldfinger*. I had to coordinate Sean's arrival at the cinema near the Arc de Triomphe with him driving the Aston-Martin DB5 and me in the passenger seat. Fortunately, there was no ejection and Connery actually made it around the notorious Arc's traffic so that we pulled up to the front of the cinema with photographers almost as numerous as the crowd. What an experience!

Paramount
(Yet Again)

Bud Ornstein announced he was leaving UA to take over European production for the newly restructured Paramount under the ownership of Charles Bluhdorn's Gulf and Western Corporation. From a beginning of cornering the coffee market in Paraguay for export (don't look too carefully, there is no proper coffee market in Paraguay), over a few years Bluhdorn morphed his Coffee Dream Factory into a multimillion-dollar conglomerate that devoured whatever it fancied. Making movies and all the glamour that came with it fascinated Bluhdorn, and his "new friend," Paramount executive Martin Davis parlayed this into his own Kingdom by the Hudson River. His great success at UA led to Ornstein being hired to run filmmaking in Europe while former actor Robert Evans was surprisingly picked to take over production at the studio.

Bluhdorn was a master at controlling those who worked for him by pitting them against each other. He had the perfect number two in Davis, who could be as deadly as a cobra in dealing with people. Bud surprisingly asked me to join his newly formed large production team as his assistant. I left UA, as the opportunity was just too great, so it was back to Paramount. I did warn Ornstein that Davis had been upset with me for leaving the company a few years earlier. However, Marty had told Bud to hire whomever he wanted if he felt they were to be of value to the operation, so with only little misgivings I left Paris for London and a big step up the corporate ladder, just a different ladder in a different corporation. I was very soon to discover that this Paramount was light-years removed from the one I left before. It was "No More Mister Nice Guy."

I was ensconced in a large office next to Bud's and given a budget to furnish as I wanted. I went Modern and it certainly looked more Californian than Chelsea. My mistake! When Marty Davis came over a few months later, he took one look and I knew I had contributed to my eventual downfall. More on that later.

When I first started I was given the task of reading countless, mostly unsolicited, scripts piled in the corner. There were what looked to be a couple of hundred, so I hired two or three part-time readers whose job was to do a synopsis and a thumbnail recommendation or rejection. Of course, it was an exercise in futility, as the films that did get made were those that came via an established producer or director with some level of interest already endorsed by one or more major acting or directing names. That was always the name of the game.

We made some winners and some losers. As long as the success ratio was one in three or four, all seemed fine—but the problem on each film in production was the same day-in, day-out nail-biting, hair-pulling exercise in anxiety and frustration at what seemed to be a never-ending challenge to one's sanity by our stateside colleagues. The demands on one's time became a joke. The problems started on our moment of arrival before 8 in the morning and accelerated with calls from New York some five hours later, when Bluhdorn et al. surfaced there, and then peaked three hours later when the studio in LA would be on the phone for whatever reason they had in the inter-cine war that existed between "them" and "us." Even when things went well there were endless problems to solve, and the sniping and back-biting between the U.S. and European production offices became a never-ending farce. In spite of all this, our European production turnout was not all bad.

*   *   *

Time has made a classic out of *The Italian Job,* and even the unsuccessful remake could not diminish the quality of our original Michael Caine hit. I was particularly involved in the selection of director Peter Collinson, as I had been responsible for Paramount picking up for distribution his small budget thriller called *The Penthouse.* We only broke even on the film, but we got Collinson signed, plus the beautiful female lead, Suzy Kendall. We showcased her talents in a film called *Fräulein Doktor,* but she didn't quite reach the potential we originally saw in her.

I guess the same held true in her personal life, as her marriage to Dudley Moore was equally short-lived. I once had occasion to be with them both in Berlin, and it was easy to tell that it was a relationship that would end sooner than later. Even if that had not been the case, his great triumph later in Hollywood with *10* would have doomed Suzy to suddenly finding herself on the outside looking in and wondering why it didn't last.

The comedic gem that was *The Italian Job* is still a worldwide hit that is a surefire success when and wherever it shows on TV. In those days, one could not show crime paying, so how to win this battle?—the plan, execution of the robbery, and the wild getaway in three Minis in the traffic of a crowded Italian metropolis. The rather hapless, somewhat pathetic band of English crooks gathered together for the ultimate "job" of thieving had to eventually lose the war by having them apprehended. Caine and his merry band were the most sympathetic audience pleasing bunch one could hope would win in the end—someway, somehow. So, in the final sequence, our heroes are seen in the large getaway van careening down a mountainous road in the Italian Alps with their large palette of gold bars. Out of control, the van comes to a shuddering halt, halfway off the road with the frightened gang huddled at the front while the gold is sliding precariously at the other end, which is hanging over eternity. What to do? Caine is at the fulcrum, trying not to upset the balance. He suddenly says to his cowering mates, "I have a great idea!" Quick cut to an exterior shot of the see-sawing vehicle, and the camera slowly pulls back to show the van teetering half way to hell (or not), as the music swells and we come to The End. What a way to finish and to send the audience home happy in thinking that all will work out fine for Caine and his merry men. Genius writing, filming and editing.

In my mind, no picture ever made had two more disparate names listed back-to-back in the cast of characters than *The Italian Job*. Try to beat the combination of Noel Coward and Benny Hill. It just can't be topped.

*   *   *

We had success with *If ...* for Albert Finney's production company (directed by Lindsay Anderson and starring Malcolm McDowell in a debut role). We just about broke even with *The Assassination Bureau*, starring Diana Rigg and Oliver Reed. I know it has been written many times, but I want to say, from my own personal perspective, that I have never met anyone who was quite so charming and entertaining while sober and such a nasty piece of work when in his cups than Reed. Lee Marvin came close, but "Ollie" won the blue ribbon in my opinion.

*   *   *

When I joined Bud's operation, Tommy Steele was just finishing a UK/U.S. co-production titled *Half a Sixpence*, based on H.G. Wells' book and the musical. Even though it was very well made (Hollywood veteran George Sidney of MGM fame was the director), it nevertheless was not a success. To paraphrase one of the hit songs, "Flash, Bang, Wallop, What a Picture!"—it wasn't!

* * *

The company spent a fortune on *Where's Jack?*, directed by a very difficult and intransigent man, James Clavell. He might have been a fine novelist (*King Rat*), but he was not a fine director. There were never-ending problems on this debacle. I lost a lot of sleep and weight with this one.

* * *

It was very pleasant to be involved with Peter O'Toole again when he made *Murphy's War* for us. I'm afraid the final film was not as pleasant for the small audiences it generated.

* * *

Bluhdorn "fell in love" with the Italian producers Dino De Laurentiis and Carlo Ponti, both old Paramount hands. Dino played him like a Stradivarius. His studio outside Rome was as grand as Hollywood's best and Paramount certainly contributed a fair share to its being competition to Cinecitta as the face of Hollywood-on-the-Tiber. I had to go to Italy on more than one occasion, but the memory that is never-ending is *Barbarella*. It was as far out as the story being filmed. Roger Vadim, Jane Fonda, et al., made for crazy times both on and off the set. Quite separately, I might be the only person to have had a meal with a *Barbarella* character, Duran(d) Duran(d) (Milo O'Shea) and the same-named rock band (minus the d's) a few years later in Paris on Bond's *A View to A Kill*. Ah, fame is fleeting!

When I was at Dino's studio, I had to visit the set of *The Taming of the Shrew* (not a Paramount picture), also being filmed there. Bud had given me a script to personally deliver to Richard Burton. It was a project close to the heart of Ornstein, and for once Paramount (both U.S. and UK) agreed it would be a perfect vehicle for Burton and Taylor. A couple of weeks later, Bud called me into his office to tell me Burton wanted to do it—but with Vanessa Redgrave as co-star! Even though he found her somewhat "cold," he felt she was better suited to the part. I often wondered if Taylor ever knew, I would have enjoyed knowing her reaction if she did. Anyway, that one died right there!

* * *

When I was in Nice, France, during the making of UA's *Love Is a Ball*, I came to know producer Martin Poll rather well. This association led to his contacting me first to offer Paramount the chance to finance his new project, *The Lion in Winter*, with Kate Hepburn and Peter O'Toole committed to star! It would have cost "small potatoes" money, but our Hollywood and New York people combined to kill it off. I was so upset, I said during one of the daily tripartite conference calls between NY, LA, and London, "Turn it down because you don't like the budget, the story matter, the casting whatever— but please don't tell me it's a No because you don't like the producer." Some of the nonsensical low budget films NY (Charley Bluhdorn) decided we would make in Italy for non-talent filmmakers (not Dino and Carlo!) were all well and good, but a surefire potential up-market hit (in my opinion) being turned down was just unfathomable to me. The silence on the phone, including Bud sitting next to me, was deafening! Another nail in my coffin.

Long after my firing, *Lion* was a critical and financial runaway hit and was nominated for the Academy Award for Best Picture, which sealed the deal for my Pyrrhic victory. Of course, this kind of victory is an aberration and has never put food on the table or helped pay the rent. As I had become a "non-person," no one called me to say I was right about the film, not that I ever felt for a second that anyone would. When you're up, you're up, and when you're down, you're down—forget it!

* * *

The Bliss of Mrs. Blossom was a delightful script that never quite lived up to its potential. The title character, played by Shirley MacLaine, is married to a brassiere-maker tycoon (Richard Attenborough) whose "thing" is pretending he is the conductor (in full uniform yet) of a marching military band in his living room while his hi-fi blasts out Souza. Shirley is up in the attic with James Booth (don't ask how he got there) and their "making it" is indicated by appropriate costumes and settings from past hit movies with a musical background that would have worked if they had been able to use the original soundtracks of the major films being parodied. All a near miss and the perfect example of a great concept not quite reaching the finish line. Pity!

Of interest is the casting. John Cleese, in his first big-screen appearance, is in a bit part as a post office counter attendant. I was on the set that day and I'm sure few initial acting jobs ever created the interest that was shown toward that Monty Python luminary.

* * *

Elvira Madigan, a Swedish film directed by the established director Bo Widerberg and with a paucity of dialogue, caused quite a stir in the art houses of the world, and a directive came in from New York to find out his availability to perhaps make a Paramount picture. I flew up to Stockholm and duly met with Widerberg. While there we also discussed possible projects with his two romantic leads from Madigan, Thommy Berggren and Pia Degermark. Bo only wanted to make very Swedish subject matter and at as small a cost as possible. Fair enough, but I don't think that was what Paramount envisaged. The beautiful Pia wasn't at all sure she even wanted to be an actress, certainly not on an international scale. Berggren was another matter. He was more than ready to travel afar and spread his wings career-wise.

Lewis Gilbert, that most venerable of screen makers, was approached by Bud to direct a very big project titled *The Adventurers*, written by one of the most prolific and successful novelists of the day, Harold Robbins. It would be filmed all over South America with a cast of thousands and a budget of many millions. However, nothing could have saved this turkey. It was also the first and only Paramount film part for our Mister Berggren. He did make one more English language picture, but he would have been far better off never leaving the land of gravlax and meatballs.

*   *   *

I had to go to Italy for Franco Zeffirelli's *Romeo and Juliet,* with the star-crossed lovers played by teenagers, as had first been written by Shakespeare. It was most impressive to observe this director at work. A real creative talent and one of the few able to combine artistry and commerciality—no easy accomplishment. I remember with much pleasure a dinner with Maggie Smith, when husband Robert Stephens was working late as the Prince of Verona. Maggie's great career is matched by her charm, wit, and candor. What American men like to call "a real man's woman." Praise indeed! A dame in both the American and British sense.

The premiere in London was a great evening, and I well remember the queen and Prince Philip impatiently waiting after finishing the star presentation lineup while Prince Charles continued to chat with our teenage Juliet, the beautiful Olivia Hussey. I think Her Majesty was not amused! All our brass had come over for the premiere and one would have thought they would have been just a little bit satisfied, but Bob Evans was about to beat out Bud Ornstein with the obvious approval and endorsement of Marty Davis (what else?—whoever won there was Marty right with him!).

The Odd Couple, Rosemary's Baby, and the soon to be released mammoth hit *Love Story* easily trumped our efforts in Europe, and their near misses with the likes of *Goodbye, Columbus, Paint Your Wagon*, and *Downhill Racer* were quickly forgotten. Even our delightful and reasonably successful *Oh! What a Lovely War* was not enough for our side and I became the first crack in the foundation of what quickly turned into Bud Ornstein's Wardour Street Waterloo. So, for me it wasn't *Goodbye Columbus*, rather Goodbye Charles Bluhdorn.

APJAC/FOX

While I was with Bud, one of the scripts commissioned was for a possible futuristic urban nightmare to be titled *Kyle*. It was still in the work phase so I was able to negotiate having the rights for two years in lieu of part of my "going away" settlement. I immediately called Arthur Jacobs, who was at that time the flavor of the year at 20th Century–Fox (*Planet of the Apes*!) and sent him the script. Within two weeks he got back to me with the news that studio head, Dick Zanuck would green light *Kyle* and I should come out to the studio immediately to go to work for APJAC as an associate on the second *Apes* about to go into production—this as a prelude to my producing *Kyle* with Jacobs as executive producer.

Arthur was happy and I was delirious—but it all turned sour in the end. It started with our having great trouble finding a director within the budget to make the picture. We discussed ad infinitum the names of various helmers and looked at countless films until eventually Arthur selected Sam Wanamaker, a very talented actor/director long based in London. He had gone to Europe at the height of the McCarthy-hysteria years, although he was most certainly not a member of the so-called Hollywood Ten. Maybe pink, but definitely not crimson. He had directed a film in the UK titled *The Executioner*, and Arthur made the final decision. It soon was obvious to me that I was not experienced or tough enough to do anything but go with the flow. The film was basically dead in the water from that point forwards, but the actual plug was pulled a few months later just before we were to start filming in the UK.

First, however, there was a fabulous visit to Montreal, where we scouted the site of its recent World's Fair and decide on the practicality of the incredible Geodesic Dome (the centerpiece of the Fair) as a setting for much of the action in our futuristic city of the mid–21st century. Now that we are actually close in real time, I think our vision was a bit ahead of itself—but that was not a consideration in the 1960s as we sat in the beautiful office of the storied mayor of Montreal, Monsieur Jean Drapeau, and agreed that we would film much of the action in his beautiful city. He treated us royally for the week we were there and I must admit, I thought of him when the project was canceled a few months later. He had been almost as enthusiastic as we were. Oh well, more's the pity. Win some, lose some.

It was back in London that the Fox London production head called me in for a meeting to announce that the project was canceled by the studio. One cannot imagine how quickly everybody, who had been beavering away to prepare for the start of filming, just disappeared from the face of "my" earth. One day they were there, the next they were gone, taken away by the plague of no more salary.

Arthur flew over, and it was obvious that our relationship had been fractured. I was found wanting, and in the highly charged business of making motion pictures, that was a no-no. It had been a heady few months being known as a Hollywood producer but, quick as a flash, I was suddenly just another out-of-work hack.

It was years later that I discovered that it was Arthur who started the close-down on the project. *Kyle* was cross-collateralized with *Apes*. This basically means that profits from an independent production company's Film One are used as a guarantee against any possible losses in a following Film Two. This was okay as long as *Kyle* might be a viable success, but when Arthur saw the project possibly spiraling out of control, that was that! Now let me be clear—Sam was Sam, but the final problem was with me. I wasn't able to do what was necessary in running the ship. It's the captain's responsibility to get the craft to safe harbor and I was already sinking in a leaking lifeboat without realizing (at the time) how I bloody well got there! APJAC already knew Film One (*Apes*) was a pot of gold and it had rapidly become clear that Film Two (*Kyle*) might just be a crock!—and there was little old me right up to my neck in the muck and mire. So, hail and farewell, my old once and sometimes friend, Arthur Powell Jacobs.

*   *   *

Two sidebars to that Fox Studio interlude—one was having a little scene shot on the grass lawn outside my office window of a boy and a girl in a passionate embrace. The film was *Myra Breckenridge*, and the very beautiful female bit player was Farrah Fawcett in only the second film of her storied Hollywood career. The second was my secretary, a very efficient young lady assigned to me from the studio office pool. She was from Arkansas, and her later rumored claim to fame was, after returning to Little Rock, briefly working for newly elected Governor Bill Clinton.

Yo-Ho, Yo-Ho, It's Off to Work I Go—Hopefully

Following my departure from APJAC, I found myself somewhat in the wilderness, although a house in the south of Spain made for a very pleasant Siberia. I had left what I obviously did best, and a separate failure meant I was now paying the price. There was little I could do but count on friends still in positions of influence to help me along the slow trip back to what could be considered regular employment in some marketing capacity.

The first step of rehabilitation was to work on a UA western to be filmed around Madrid and Almeria (Spain's Old West location) titled *The Spikes Gang*. Thanks to UA's Fred Goldberg and Gabe Sumner, I had at least got my toe back on the yellow brick road. It was to be produced by Walter Mirisch and directed by Richard Fleischer, who I knew socially from Hollywood, thanks to Arthur Jacobs. It was to star one of the very top names of the day, Lee Marvin. He had a fierce reputation and I knew I quickly had to let him be aware I was not in fear of him. Instead of dropping the big names with whom I had previously worked, I let him know that my combat World War II service was just as "bad" as his and that took him by surprise. We got along famously. The "gang" of the title was three teenagers, one of whom was the famous Richie of *Happy Days*, Ron Howard. He had started acting at the age of six in TV's *The Andy Griffith Show*. His big screen career took off via *The Music Man* and, a little over a decade later, *American Graffiti*. Of note is that one of the other members of the Spikes Gang was played by another *American Graffiti* alumnus, Charles Martin Smith. Howard was but a few years away from becoming one of the most creative and enduring of film directors. He deserved his success.

Marvin had a reputation for being a heavy drinker and a problem on the set. My take on this was based on an incident during *Spikes*. If Lee wanted time off or to have whatever he considered important done, he started drinking, knowing full well he would get his way eventually if he became too soused to remember his lines. So, the longer it took to get his way, the more loaded

The author (left) and happy landings with Lee Marvin (right) and his wife, production manager Tom Pevsner (second from left) and producer Walter Mirisch (center) at the Madrid airport to shoot *The Spikes Gang* for UA, 1973.

and out of it he became. If one considers this the actions of a spoiled child, so be it. He was not the first actor to be impossible and he won't be the last. It comes with the territory!

One footnote—Marvin was outrageous at the best of times, but his far-out behavior was almost always calculated, in my opinion. As an example, Barbara Barker, my publicity assistant on the film (and future star European correspondent for *W.* and *Women Wear Daily*), had invited out to the set the very serious and somewhat up-tight Associated Press representative for Spain. During the lunch break, Marvin, who was in a contretemps with Mirisch at the time, put on his disrespectful behavior hat and announced in his booming baritone to the astonished AP man, with all the cast and crew seated nearby, "I don't believe you have met my wife, the best fuck in Hollywood." The newspaper man wanted to jump out of his chair and be anywhere but where he was—with crazy Hollywood film people. All of us were taken aback by how far Lee went this time. Needless to say, no publicity resulted that day, thank God.

*   *   *

I was in constant communication with Bud Ornstein, by now out at Paramount and briefly with Warner Bros. Through his actions, I was asked by Cubby Broccoli if I was available to be the publicity director on the second Roger Moore Bond film, *The Man with the Golden Gun*. Harry and Cubby were nearing the end of their association and the first step had been that Harry carried the producer load on the previous picture, *Live and Let Die*, and had his own personally selected PR honcho on that one. Now it was Cubby's turn to have the final word on Who's Who and What's What, chez 007. My being reunited with the franchise was primarily thanks to the good offices of Bud—he always felt bad about what happened to me at Paramount, though certainly was not his fault.

I was back in business, literally and figuratively, so it was off to London and New York, then on to Hong Kong and later Bangkok for the location shoots. In New York I met Maud Adams, who was to play the second female lead. She was very special in every way (and richly deserved to be brought back by Cubby as the feminine star in *Octopussy*). Britt Ekland, a fellow Swede, would catch up with us in Hong Kong along with Roger Moore, Christopher Lee, and the rest of the cast. I arrived there in advance of Moore, as I had to organize the press for his arrival. I well remember meeting for the first time Roger's fiery Italian wife, Luisa, who was already ensconced in a most palatial suite at the storied Peninsula Hotel with their second son, just a baby then. On the floor above was the Philippines' Imelda Marcos, who was there for a bit of shopping (shoes?) with an entourage of some fifty retainers. What a way to go! She was most gracious and charming when she met our group.

Luisa was an absolute delight and we hit it off from the start. Never a bad thing to get along with the spouse of the star. Anyway, she was a Dr. Jekyll and "Mrs." Hyde character when it came to Roger. In the years I was around this happy yet embattled pair, I never could tell when there would be a blow-up coming. Of course, one can never ever know what any marriage is like when the doors are closed. The bottom line is that I truly liked both Roger and Luisa as individuals; when together one was always on thin ice as to which way to go.

The author (right) with (from left) co-star Maud Adams, producer Albert "Cubby" Broccoli, director Guy Hamilton and actor Hervé Villechaize (back to camera) at the *The Man with the Golden Gun* pre-production press event, Bangkok, 1973 (*The Man with the Golden Gun* ©1974 Danjaq, LLC, and Metro-Goldwyn-Mayer Studios Inc. All Rights Reserved).

During the filming of *Goldfinger*, I had only been introduced to director Guy Hamilton, so it was a pleasure to get to know this most cultured and urbane English gentleman. Having already established a close rapport with Maud, I guess I inadvertently gave our feminine lead, the very beautiful Britt Ekland, the impression my publicity efforts would be more favorable to her unknown Swedish compatriot. Not my intention, but a rift was established without a doubt. A motion picture company on a distant location can make for a fractious environment where feelings and sensibilities can wear very thin very quickly.

I really enjoyed my time on *Gun* and particularly came to know and like Christopher Lee. Though usually serious, he had a delightful sense of humor and was a thoroughly decent human being and also a world class raconteur. During the release when we were all on a promotional tour of the

States, two incidents stand out. One was in the lobby of our hotel in Atlanta. As the lift doors opened, a "good old Georgia boy" waiting to go up saw Lee and shouted at the top of his voice, "Dracula! Right on!" Naturally we all broke up at Chris's embarrassment. Even his lovely wife, Gitte, couldn't hide her amusement at his momentary discomfort. It truly was a funny moment in time.

The other happening was again in a hotel. This time the Sherry-Netherland in New York City. Chris and I had got up at the crack of dawn for his appearance on ABC's *Good Morning America*. We had returned to the hotel and, no longer out in public, had each taken our golden guns from our waist bands, the one solid and the other the assembled pen, lighter, and cuff-links that Lee's character Scaramanga uses to threaten Bond and which he was constantly assembling for fascinated TV hosts wherever we were. We were walking down the hallway to the suite, each carrying a golden gun, when a door opened and a hand reached out to collect that morning's news-paper. A robed Billy Wilder, who knew us both, took one look and, with razor-sharp quickness, said in his best World War II German-Jewish accent,

With my longtime friend Christopher Lee (left) (photograph by Gitte Lee, author's collection).

150

"You vudn't shoot an elderly Jew, vud you?" We both almost joined the *Times* on the hallway floor as we collapsed in laughter.

Following the tour, it was briefly back to Spain, as there would be a hiatus before the next 007 would be made and I was not (yet) a permanent employee. Cubby was not about to pay me for just sitting in a London office. I happily caught on briefly with yet another film company. The Columbia Pictures production office in London wanted me to oversee the publicity on two films. One was *Bobby Deerfield*, produced and directed by the most accomplished Sydney Pollack. This was a physiological take on a racing car driver and was to be filmed in Italy and France. Al Pacino, one of the biggest stars at that time, had the title role and the lovely Swiss, Marthe Keller, was the leading lady. I went down to very picturesque Bellagio on Lake Como, where I found Mr. Pacino very hard going. His manner toward me was very surly. He really didn't want any distraction to "acting" (fair enough). On each of the few visits to the set during those two or three days, I had to be re-introduced to him as if I had never met him before. He is still one of our finest actors and I like to think that years have made him PR-savvy. I have met many others who were "difficult" in their own way but, for me, Mister Pacino of that time takes the *pannetone*.

The other film was *The Last Woman*, shot in Paris by the cerebral Italian director Marco Ferreri, and starring Gérard Depardieu and the beautiful Ornella Muti. They all spoke excellent English. Why can't monolingual Anglo Saxons be so linguistically accomplished? The subject matter was a real throw of the dice when it came to public acceptance. Any film about a man who, in a moment of madness, removes his most private appendage with an electric bread knife is about as graphic and disturbing as it gets. When the film opened and closed with great rapidity some months later, I had already finished my short stint at Columbia, but that didn't prevent me saying the obvious to my fellow show business *confrèrs*—"The film obviously needed cutting."

Thanks to Pollack, I later joined his pre-production team for the next film on his schedule to be set around Pamplona, Spain, and its annual running of the bulls. We went to the next fiesta for scouting and some second unit filming with a very small crew. A few days in that madness was enough for any person, believe me. The project never got made; however, those four days will always be remembered with awe, and to have actually done The Run is yet another of those "whatever did I do wrong to be HERE" moments.

Universal

Through relationships made while at UA and Paramount over the years, I was offered the number two job at Universal in New York. Two fellow publicity executives had become heads there in LA and I was tapped. Universal was an exception to the rule in that the company power base was at the studio and not the East Coast.

While there, I handled the premiere of *Slap Shot* in New Haven, Connecticut, where Paul Newman was the star turn. He could not have been friendlier or more cooperative. He was obviously on his home turf.

A low budget film shot in New York was titled *Heroes*. It starred Henry Winkler of "Fonzie" fame. A thoroughly nice guy. Of interest in a small part was the not yet famous Harrison Ford, while in just a bit part was the not-yet-discovered Danny DeVito.

A film titled *The Seduction of Joe Tynan* was filmed around New York sites and is of note because of a scene I actually observed being filmed in a well-known lower Park Avenue watering hole. This is worth comment because of an attractive blonde newcomer sitting at the bar in one of her earlier appearances on the big screen. Her name—Meryl Streep.

I had to be up at Hyannis Port, Massachusetts, for the filming of the second *Jaws* film and spent many days at West Point in connection with the Premiere of *MacArthur*. There was always much to be done and it was certainly a busy time. I was beginning to realize why I was offered the job.

* * *

Of all the pictures I was involved with at Universal, the most time consuming—and frustrating—was *The Wiz*, an all-black casting of *The Wizard of Oz* which had been a really big Broadway musical hit. Even with Sidney Lumet at the helm, it was doomed the minute Diana Ross was signed to play Dorothy. A twelve-year-old innocent she wasn't! Also cast was one of the most "far out" people I ever met. Michael Jackson might have been one of America's greatest entertainers, but he added little to the proceedings as the Scarecrow. To me he was downright scary.

For once I was the one in a position to help a fellow publicist from days past. I hired Saul Cooper, whose ability was only matched by his warmth and intellect. The words "gentle" and "man" together truly captured the personality of this rare bird in the film business. Of special interest is that he had just finished working for Cubby on *The Spy Who Loved Me*. There were two or three unforgettable happenings from *The Wiz*. Every opportunity to cause trouble happened and it became almost a battleground. As for Diana Ross, I personally did not find her "supreme" in any way, shape, or form. The amazing thing in all this turmoil was to observe Sidney Lumet go along his merry way directing the movie without seeming to be affected by all the rancor going on day in, day out. After all, he was not the producer!

A memory from that film was being on the set in one of Universal's warehouses on the West Side of New York, where the sequence was filmed in which Lena Horne (in her last screen appearance) played a celestial Glenda (the Good Witch), singing with a background of dozens of clouds with a little black child's face peering out from each cotton-like cocoon of all things bright and beautiful.

The Wiz was a flop and Universal's original concept of having a hit like *Stormy Weather* or *Carmen Jones* didn't happen. *The Wiz*" was No-Wiz!

The events of 9/11 brought back to me vivid memories of the nighttime location shoots at the World Trade Center. The esplanade between the towers was turned into the Emerald City, and it was one of the best examples of movie magic in concept, design, and execution. Over the week of night filming, Lumet had invited New York–like film luminaries to bring their children to watch the filming. Among the visitors were Tony Perkins and his wife, Bernie Berenson, and their daughter. I well remember their couple of visits when I saw her name listed as a victim in one of the crashed planes. An eerie coincidence of the worst kind possible.

*   *   *

I was content at Universal, but when the opportunity came about to return to the Bond operation, I bade farewell to New York yet again and was soon flying back to Europe and ten years of employment that was as great at the end of my career as the early years at Paramount in Hollywood were for me at the beginning.

Bond Forevermore

Moonraker had been announced as the next 007 production in the pipeline, so toward the latter part of *The Wiz* shoot, Saul Cooper and I discussed the situation. While Saul obviously wanted the gig, he also needed to remain in New York at that time for family reasons. Cubby had made it clear he would welcome me back, but that Saul was in first position since he had worked on *The Spy Who Loved Me*. We came up with what we hoped Cubby would accept as a solution. I would go to Europe to oversee the production and world distribution from there, and Saul would be in charge of the USA, the major financial market, and also to be a constant publicity presence in dealing with UA. This was always a most important factor and not to be taken lightly by any independent producer, much less one with the world's biggest film franchise on his hands. A trip to New York by Broccoli on Bond business gave the three of us the opportunity to talk about matters in person at Cubby's beautiful Upper East Side brownstone, and we quickly worked out a position favorable to us all. Of course, once Cubby agreed to our concept, UA had little option but to accept what was basically a *fait accompli*.

Everyone thought that *Moonraker* would be made at Pinewood, but the size of the space station as conceived by one of the greatest of all set designers, Ken Adam, made even the facilities at Pinewood inadequate. The answer was a three-tier construction at the Les Studios d'Épinay in Paris, so the entire operation was moved to France. An unexpected plus for those of us charged with selling the film was the casting of Richard Kiel to play Jaws, the giant henchman of the villain Drax. Kiel became almost as important in the publicizing of the film as Roger Moore. He had created quite a stir in the previous film, but that was a minor appearance. In *Moonraker* he was right up there at the top of the tree. Jaws became the iconic Bond henchmen in the same way that Goldfinger will historically be the favorite Bond baddie.

Filming in Venice is relatively easier during the winter off-season (tourists at a minimum), although weather is the problem. Sure enough, there were a few days when it was not the easiest getting around with water ankle deep in some of the streets and squares. UA brought in a very large group of journalists from all over the world to watch some of the filming, and there we were in the middle of St. Mark's Square after gathering to observe the scene where Moore is in the motorized (for the land) gondola being chased by the baddies. He had just left the set for the lunch break and I was getting all the press together for a visit to one of the better restaurants, when suddenly there was Luisa in our midst. For some reason she thought Roger would be there for her to join him for the cast and crew lunch. A minor mix-up but the volatile Signora Moore, realizing she was playing to a very large international gathering, some of whom were busily snapping away with their Nikons and Canons, loudly announced in her marvelous Italian-accented

Richard Kiel (left) and I hit the ground running on the *Moonraker* promotional tour, 1979 (*Moonraker* © 1979 Danjaq, LLC, and Metro-Goldwyn-Mayer Studios Inc. All Rights Reserved).

voice, "Jerry, you ah-see Roger, you tell-a heem to go fookah heemself!" I quickly pointed her in the direction of the crew lunch site and pretended nothing was ever said!

The location outside Paris at the fabled Château de Vaux-le-Vicomte was magical and the month we filmed in Rio was for me what working on a Bond film was all about. It truly was, quite often, a veritable "Alice in Wonderland" experience. I was so happy to be back on board the gravy train that was James Bond. Work hard, keep the wheels turning and well oiled (thanks to the world's media!), and just sit back and enjoy the ride!

The premiere in Paris was a big success and at the Bois de Boulogne dinner afterwards I found myself at the same table as one Mohamed El-Fayed. His son Dodi was at the famous Le Rosey school in Switzerland with Cubby and Dana's teenage daughter Barbara, who had worked with us in the publicity department when not at her studies. She became like a beloved niece to me and I treasure her friendship to this day.

Barbara Broccoli peers through the camera lens while wearing a prop Russian army winter hat on location for *The Living Daylights*, 1986 (*The Living Daylights* © 1987 Danjaq, LLC, and Metro-Goldwyn-Mayer Studios Inc. All Rights Reserved).

A special showing in Strasbourg was another high spot and we flew a large contingent in on a chartered plane. I was personally delighted that *Moonraker*, preceded by *The Spy Who Loved Me*, showed that Lewis Gilbert was still one of the very best of directors. With these two Bond films, he put *The Adventurers* well behind him and set sail for future hits like *Educating Rita* and *Shirley Valentine*.

Of all the tours I would make around the world for different James Bond films, the one that Corinne Clery, Richard Kiel, and I made to South Africa has to be the most unusual. We found ourselves at MalaMala, the famous wild animal game reserve "hotel" in the fabled Kruger National Park. The beautiful Clery, famed for starring in the controversial French hit *The Story of O*, was about as cooperative and successful at achieving newspaper space and TV appearances as she was at creating sensuous and captivating screen characters. It didn't hurt that her English was as perfect as her Italian and

The author (left), all aboard the *Moonraker* European press tour, with key cast and crew members. Roger Moore (center) admires his likeness in the back as Richard Kiel towers over all (*Moonraker* © 1979 Danjaq, LLC, and Metro-Goldwyn-Mayer Studios Inc. All Rights Reserved).

German. This made this beautiful French actress one of the most successful of all the major Bond personalities I squired around the world. A sidebar to the MalaMala visit—while there, who walked into the bar in the back of beyond but George Hamilton. I had got to know him back in my Paris days when he made *Viva Maria* with Brigitte Bardot and Jeanne Moreau for Paramount. After a day with lions and other wild things, an evening with the likes of George Hamilton and Corinne Clery was almost too much of a good thing!

The publicity operation as envisaged by Saul and I worked perfectly, and I suddenly found myself becoming a permanent member of the EON team, although for administrative purposes, I actually was employed by another of Cubby's companies, Warfield Productions Inc. Michael Wilson, Dana's son

Michael G. Wilson (center) and a local boatman (left) with the author during the Florida shoot (doubling for Brazil) on *Moonraker*, 1978 (*Moonraker* © 1979 Danjaq, LLC, and Metro-Goldwyn-Mayer Studios Inc. All Rights Reserved).

by her first marriage, was a fine lawyer and worked out all the details. He was as laid back in personality as he was quietly forceful in the workplace. Combined with a great intellect and a penchant for writing, he became very quickly the obvious heir apparent (along with Barbara) to the Bond franchise. Today Michael is in place with Barbara as the present generation running the 007 empire. After more than fifty years and twenty-four films (at the time of writing), who's to say there won't be diamond 75th anniversary for 007 in the future. After all, to paraphrase Mister Fleming, "Bonds are forever."

*   *   *

The next to be made was *For Your Eyes Only* and as we were to be back at Pinewood. I was able to set what became a relatively permanent team. With the very best unit publicist in the UK, Geoff Freeman, to handle the day-in, day-out production publicity and two of the top production still photographers, Keith Hamshere and George Whitear, on the first and second units, respectively, we formed a formidable group worthy of the franchise.

Veteran Bond unit photographer Keith Hamshere (left) and Ian Fleming Foundation co-founder Doug Redenius (right) with the author at the launch party for *Some Kind of Hero*, London, 2015 (Redenius collection).

Keith was an exception to the rule of most people in our end of the movie business in that he had been a major child star on the West End stage until he literally was too old for what he did so well, but he will always be known as the very first *Oliver*. He was a large talent in a very small frame. George was as reliable as only a veteran of countless films could be and got on with everybody, not always easy for someone whose job is to "get the picture" without being obvious. As for Geoff Freeman, he was unparalleled in getting whomever to do the necessary to the maximum with a minimum of fuss. While I felt that Roger liked me, at least when things were going well, he loved Geoff, and with reason! Of all the British publicists I worked with from 1956 to 1990, Freeman was, quite simply, the best.

For Your Eyes Only was notable for being the first big directorial effort of former film editor and second unit director John Glen. His filming of the now iconic ski-slope parachute jump off the mountain top in *Spy* earned Broccoli's admiration and a decision to award his talent by giving him his well and justly earned director's stripes. The location in Corfu and the Greek mainland were memorable to me for several reasons. One was the problems with the Greek Orthodox priests in their Meteora mountaintop churches.

Posing with Bond title designer Maurice Binder (center) and longtime UK unit publicist Geoff Freeman (right) in the woods of Buckinghamshire during *The Living Daylights* shoot, 1986 (*The Living Daylights* © 1987 Danjaq, LLC, and Metro-Goldwyn-Mayer Studios Inc. All Rights Reserved).

One problem after another in order for the filming to proceed was thrown at us. A bit part by an actor named Charles Dance in the beach buggy chase pre-dated his future stardom that came a couple of years down the road with the giant TV hit, *The Jewel in the Crown*. Topol was as friendly and agreeable a person as one could hope to be with, and we took advantage of his presence during the distribution publicity tours. A lovely man!

I had championed the beautiful French actress Carole Bouquet to play the female lead and Cubby never let me forget it. She was good in the part of Melina and no more of a problem than any actress, but her then husband was a constant thorn in the side of all concerned on the production. Another unplanned problem was on finding out that Tula, one of our beautiful Bond ladies (in the standard issue swimming pool scene), had been born a fella. When it became public news much later it didn't really matter but, at the time, it was a bit disconcerting, I must admit. I should point out that we insiders called these lovelies, who with never ending regularity peopled the films of that time, "Bond Girls." The female lead was the "leading lady" or "star." The media, however, called them all "Bond Girls" and that hasn't changed as of this writing. Let's face it, whether an actress or model was starring, in a second lead (certain to be dispatched sooner or later), in just a bit part, or as a prominent extra in but one scene, the media called her a "Bond Girl" FOREVER!

My main memory of *Eyes Only* was the Corfu location where my wife and I became friendly with the lovely Cassandra Harris, who played the ill-fated Countess Lisl. She was a truly special person and proved to be of great value to us in promoting the film, particularly in Australia and New Zealand. Her husband was an incredibly handsome young Irish actor who hadn't yet "made it." He couldn't have been more loving and attentive of Cassie, and I would never feel less admiration for Pierce Brosnan than I did from those early days when he was truly a nobody. More on Pierce later.

A final footnote on the use of a Citroen 2CV for one of the big car chases—this was an amusing counterpoint to the gadget-filled super sports cars that went in the films before.

*　*　*

With UA's Australian publicity director (left) and the lovely Cassandra Harris, then-wife of Pierce Brosnan, at an event Down Under for *For Your Eyes Only*, 1981 (UA/UIP Australia, *For Your Eyes Only* © 1981 Danjaq, LLC, and Metro-Goldwyn-Mayer Studios Inc. All Rights Reserved).

From the day that *Octopussy* was announced as the next 007, there was an understandable furor in the English language press over the overtly sexual innuendo of the title. Little matter that it had been around since being the title of one of Ian Fleming's short stories. The media, always at its happiest whenever able to second-guess anything or anybody famous, was checkmated by the sheer volume of usage and it eventually became no more controversial than a saucy seaside postcard.

It was delightful to have Maud Adams back, and as the star in the title role! Great for her and for us charged with the task of selling the new Bond. Life was good if you worked at it. Handling all public relations matters for the James Bond franchise was about as good as it could get. With Cubby at my back there was little I could not deal with and come out smelling like a rose—you had to *just always be right*!

It was a heady time! To walk into the main office of ad/pub at United Artists as a senior vice-president of Cubby's Warfield Productions and be treated with respect and a little awe for the position I held was an appealing experience. It was about as rare as successfully growing a black orchid! Being party to UA's most important and profitable production company went more than a little way in helping ensure *their* own employment longevity at UA. Glory is great, even when one knows it is but the reflection of something far bigger than you are.

After many of the UK scenes involving the circus, the train, and the airfield (with the incredible midget AcroStar Jet) were filmed, Roger, Maud, the veteran Louis Jourdan and the rest of the main cast went to West Germany for the Checkpoint Charlie scenes plus other exteriors to complete the circus and train sequences. It was quite something to observe actor Steven Berkoff up close. He was one of the most serious actors I ever watched and he gave a new meaning to the word "intensive."

The whole kit and kaboodle then flew to India for weeks of very hot and humid location work. To be based in a fabulous new hotel that was part of the Maharana of Udaipur's palace on the shores of Lake Pichola, in the fabled city of Udaipur in Rajasthan, was a once in a lifetime experience. The crew was across the water in the famed Udaipur Hotel, situated on a small island smack dab in the middle of the lake. I always had to be quartered near Moore, so I wondered for once, did I have the best deal? It was one of those rare times being a very minor part of the top-whack was not necessarily the best. If the middle of the lake was good enough for the producer and the director, it certainly would have been good enough for the likes of me!

Sometimes a publicist just has to clean up shit ... but at least it's show business! With Geoff Freeman (right) on location in India for *Octopussy*, 1982 (*Octopussy* © 1983 Danjaq, LLC, and Metro-Goldwyn-Mayer Studios Inc. All Rights Reserved).

Taking a break with Maud Adams during the *Octopussy* shoot (men in front unidentified), India, 1982 (*Octopussy* © 1983 Danjaq, LLC, and Metro-Goldwyn-Mayer Studios Inc. All Rights Reserved).

The tiger hunt and the big festival procession meant "elephants galore," and I couldn't help but think back to my earlier days at Paramount and *Elephant Walk*. There's a famous joke about a circus worker shoveling elephant "do-do" who responds, when asked if he was happy in his work, "I always wanted to be in show business." Well, make of it what you will, I was being very handsomely rewarded and with not a broom in sight!

J and Q: With actor Desmond Lewellyn (right), southern England, 1990s (author's collection).

"Some days are better than others..." With the lovely *Octopussy* women (*Octopussy* © 1983 Danjaq, LLC, and Metro-Goldwyn-Mayer Studios Inc. All Rights Reserved).

Two footnotes to the India shoot. One was getting to know the great tennis star Vijay Amritraj, who played an assistant to Q. Vijay was a delightful man and a most pleasant counterpoint to the demands and needs of actors. Speaking of Q, I should mention Desmond Llewelyn, about as nice a man as I ever met in all my years in the business. Though his total screen time in all his combined Bond appearances amounted to only a few minutes, the hours he spent helping publicize the films all over the world was monumental. He never ever complained and I came to value his friendship to the end. His tragic traffic death was a great personal loss to one and all.

Our Bond Girls came into their own in India as major members of Octopussy's female army. Mary Stavin (former Miss World), Carole Ashby, and Alison Worth, to name but three, proved of major help in the "selling" phase with their most important contribution in promoting more than one Bond screen appearance. All who toured for us were unsung heroes in selling the various films, be it Europe, South and Central America, the United States, or Australasia and the Far East, there they were to be found doing their greater good in promoting all things 007. All the problems keeping them ready and on time, plus herding them through airports and in and out of hotels and restaurants paled in comparison to what their presence achieved for us in media exposure. The years may pass and nature takes its inevitable toll, but they will always be those beauties at their most fruitful to me. Bless them, each and every one. I loved them all.

*   *   *

When I learned that *A View to a Kill* would feature major locations in Paris and San Francisco, I was overjoyed. What a plus for me to be in Paris again for more than just a few days and also to get back to Northern California. My civilian life post–World War II began there and my career in the motion picture industry certainly started there, so returning for the film's major location shoot in the City by the Bay was a source of much personal satisfaction.

In Paris, we filmed around and on the Eiffel Tower, while the horse sequences were shot in suburban Chantilly. I had never been to the Château or the fabled horse museum before so that was most interesting. The principal villain was played by the brilliant Oscar winner Christopher Walken. He was great fun to be around and was the life of every evening's after-filming crew party. Amazingly, he never was the worse for wear the next morning and he was letter-perfect with his dialogue and always "hit his mark" in all his scenes. A thorough professional.

An American in Paris: Striking the 007 pose under the Eiffel Tower during the *A View to a Kill* shoot, 1984 (*A View to a Kill* © 1985 Danjaq, LLC, and Metro-Goldwyn-Mayer Studios Inc. All Rights Reserved).

The author (left) on location with Cubby Broccoli (second from left), Roger Moore and Dana Broccoli during the *A View to a Kill* shoot, Paris, 1984 (*A View to a Kill* ©1985 Danjaq, LLC, and Metro-Goldwyn-Mayer Studios Inc. All Rights Reserved).

One night in Paris, Roger, Chris, and I spent a great time in the bars and byways that was every bit the equal of an earlier evening in "Gay Paree" with O'Toole and Burton. Roger loved all things Italian and I really came to know the delights of grappa that night. You can say what you like about movie stars but, boy, most know how to live!

Grace Jones was quite something, one of the great characters of all time. Love her or hate her, she was certainly a one-off, and I am happy to say she was relatively cooperative with me, although I had to be very cautious in word and deed. Her volatility was an awesome and fearsome thing to behold. Her very young son was with her and she was every inch the doting and caring Mum when not "on." I liked Grace, but working with her was somewhat akin to the men who planted dynamite to blow holes in tunnels and mountainsides. Be very careful how you went about your work! She had an incredibly handsome Swedish "hunk" with her. His relaxation was running backwards, and it was quite something to observe the Parisians near our hotel as he whizzed by them only to be facing them after he passed. Their amazed reaction was most amusing as they literally couldn't tell immediately if he was coming or going! Dolph Lundgren only did a very small bit in *View*, but he was soon to become one of the very top motion picture action heroes.

The Eiffel Tower sequences were magical and the paraglide leap off the top was on a par with the car jump over the Klong River in Thailand for *Golden Gun*. You stood there and couldn't quite believe what you just saw. It is no secret that the Bond films of those years brought a new meaning to "pushing the envelope." Staying ahead of the competition was but one of Cubby's many strengths. The skiing sequences were outstanding and the stunts were the best part of one of the lesser successful 007 outings.

Patrick Macnee was as warm and friendly in real life as he appeared to be in his acting persona. He was a great trouper, and he did yeoman duty in the foreign tours promoting the film, always with a smile and good humor. He was, like Llewelyn, one of a very rare breed.

The members of the famous band Duran Duran were most helpful, and their specially filmed title song shot on the Eiffel Tower was great for the film. They were also an integral part of our San Francisco premiere activity that took place in the cinema in the city's Palace of Fine Arts, unchanged from my first visit there as a preschooler. I also got a charge out of the big action sequence in the picture when San Francisco's City Hall is "on fire." I

Roger Moore (left) and I catch some Z's in Norway, 1985 (UA/UIP Sweden).

reflected on being in that building on another school tour some fifty years earlier. More "full circle" moments for me.

Of all the countless tours I made around the world, one of the most personally satisfying was a visit to Norway for *View*. Roger Moore brought his fine young son Geoffrey along and, as photographic appeal, we had the absolutely delightful Fiona Fullerton. Everything that could go right happened, and at the end of a week's work it was all capped off with a sailboat trip up into one of the magnificent Norwegian fjords. A magical day and a perfect example of "The Joy of Promoting Bond." It didn't always happen, but when it did, the tours were awesome—Cubby et al. in the Ginza of Tokyo. Roger Moore everywhere. Bond lovelies at a bullfight in Madrid or in the Andes of Peru. On a Chinese junk off Hong Kong with Desmond Llewelyn. In the Australian Outback with Patrick Macnee and Tanya Roberts. The jungle of South Africa with Richard Kiel and Corinne Clery. The skyscrapers of Chicago with Timothy Dalton. The beaches of Rio with Lynn-Holly Johnson. Sydney Harbor with Cassandra Harris and Topol. Wherever there were newspapers, magazines, or radio and TV stations, there we were with some permutation of Bond personalities spreading the mantra of one very special secret agent to a waiting world. The very finest hotel and restaurant was but one of the perks, and I always wondered which I preferred, the making of

Roger Moore throws out a line on a Norwegian fjord during a break in the *A View to a Kill* press tour (UA/UIP Sweden, *A View to a Kill* © 1985 Danjaq, LLC, and Metro-Goldwyn-Mayer Studios Inc. All Rights Reserved).

My thousand-air-mile stare on the *Moonraker* tour. Note writer Christopher Wood reading a newspaper (*Moonraker* © 1979 Danjaq, LLC, and Metro-Goldwyn-Mayer Studios Inc. All Rights Reserved).

each film in some exotic locale or the release campaigns in equally fascinating corners of the globe. There is a business class and a first class, but you haven't traveled until you've gone Bond Class!

When it came to selling a film, no one in the promotional field could hope for a more professional and cooperative star than Moore. He was truly a publicist's dream, and it was only on the rarest of occasions that he turned down a request for his time. I knew that in writing about Bond I would inevitably have to use the phrase "Nobody does it better," but that does capture the late Roger Moore to a T. Not only better, but he did it EVERYWHERE!

* * *

Like a fine wine that can't be left open forever the shelf life of the actor playing Bond comes to an inevitable end for one reason or another. It was painful for all concerned when the time came for Roger to say "Aloha," but that was his decision. So be it. With Pierce Brosnan standing in the wings, we all felt secure that while one King Is Dead, Long Live the Next One. But,

The author (left) in yet another country, another airport with Roger Moore (right) on the *Moonraker* press tour, 1979. (UIP photograph, *Moonraker* © 1979 Danjaq, LLC, and Metro-Goldwyn-Mayer Studios Inc. All Rights Reserved).

as with Edward the Seventh, there was an American spanner in the works for the James Bond franchise! It came in the person of the head of NBC in New York, who felt that Cubby Broccoli would have to accept that the actor playing James Bond could also continue to star in a TV series playing Remington Steele. How little he knew Cubby!

It was all so heartbreaking for Pierce and Cassie, and I was there with them in Los Angeles when the plug was pulled. That was one very unhappy time for all. As someone once said, "That's show business." I'm happy to reflect that, for once, all was well that ended well and the extra four years during Timothy Dalton's tenure were, in my humble opinion, to Pierce's advantage when he finally did step out into the iris of the gun barrel and fire the trusty Walther PPK on Pinewood's Stage Four.

There were many who were to be considered to play Bond, but one really was head and shoulders above the rest. Dalton was ruggedly tall, handsome, British, and a remarkably fine actor. I remembered his work in *The Lion in Winter*, and when we met in Cubby's office after he signed his contract, I quickly realized that Dalton was not only very serious about his profession, but that he was someone who reluctantly accepted that publicity and promotion had to be a necessary part of being James Bond. It would certainly have to be endured, if not embraced, in the process. He was in uncharted waters and one can't blame him for being cautious at the time. Once he learned we were not the enemy, he became awesome in his cooperation. While Tim was friendly enough on the surface at the start, it was quite obvious that the Roger Moore days were well and truly over. Connery and Bond came to life as one and grew together. Dalton was faced with not only two more incantations in the role, but all that had happened over twenty-five years. It was new territory for Tim and was equally so for those of us at EON who had developed a routine modus operandi, not of complacency, but of execution and expectation.

"Everyone who was anyone" from *The Living Daylights*: from left, Maryam d'Abo, Timothy Dalton, Barbara Broccoli, Cubby Broccoli, Dana Broccoli, John Glen and his wife, Janine, and the author at the Deauville Film Festival, 1987 (UIP France, *The Living Daylights* © 1987 Danjaq, LLC, and Metro-Goldwyn-Mayer Studios Inc. All Rights Reserved).

Five years and two films later when I retired, I not only considered Tim a friend (rarely achieved between actors and PR types), but really felt that he had been a fine addition to the Bond saga and a worthy contributor to its continuing success.

Production on *The Living Daylights* started on top of the Rock of Gibraltar and moved across the straits for scenes in Tangier. This was followed by filming in the old French Foreign Legion outpost of Ouarzazate in the Atlas Mountains area of Morocco. I came to know two of my very favorite Bond cast members during that time. Maryam d'Abo was a truly lovely girl and her acting was more than matched by her sweetness and charm. To me she was sort of a junior-grade Audrey Hepburn (not bad, not bad!). While never achieving the heights of Miss H, Maryam certainly came close, at least on a personal level in the eyes of this poor purveyor of publicity who had the good fortune to know them both. Mentioning dear Audrey naturally makes me think of the Netherlands, and that is an obvious segue to my other 007 favorite, Jeroen Krabbe. He was a consummate professional and went on to

At Pinewood, setting up a number of original Bond props for a *Life Magazine* photo shoot celebrating *The Living Daylights*, 1986 (*The Living Daylights* © 1987 Danjaq, LLC, and Metro-Goldwyn-Mayer Studios Inc. All Rights Reserved).

a solid acting career in the States far from the canals and windmills of his native land. On a promotional tour when we opened *Daylights* in Amsterdam, he was literally lionized by the media and public alike. A sidebar—he is an even better painter than actor. Jeroen is truly blessed with talent.

Our location in Austria was a startling change of locale after the heat of North Africa, and Vienna was as *Gemültlichtkeit* as it was advertised. If there was an iconic site, we filmed a scene in front of it. I had hoped for a brief homage of sorts to *The Third Man*, one of my all-time favorite movies. No such luck (aside from a scene in the amusement park at the Prater). However, I did find the famous doorway where the light came on to suddenly show Orson Welles standing among the shadows. A magical moment for a movie maven!

The high spot of our filming back at Pinewood was the royal visit of Prince Charles and Princess Diana. I am proud to have suggested the break-a-way bottle idea for a surefire worldwide publicity result. Diana really

TRH visit "The Living Daylights"

Pinewood Studios
DEC . 11, 1986

Odeon Leicester Square
JUNE 29, 1987

Didn't hurt a bit: Princess Diana smashes a (fake) bottle on Prince Charles' head on a visit to Pinewood (© 1987 Danjaq, LLC, and Metro-Goldwyn-Mayer Studios Inc. All Rights Reserved).

Meeting Princess Diana in the receiving line at the *A View to a Kill* royal premiere, London, June 14, 1985 (*A View to a Kill* © 1985 Danjaq, LLC, and Metro-Goldwyn-Mayer Studios Inc. All Rights Reserved).

enjoyed the moment and Charles, a prince who could really be charming—when in a good mood—sportingly went along with letting his wife whack him over the head with a fake bottle. Truly a good time was had by all and the prince actually mentioned it to me when I was in the receiving line, one of three or four of which I was fortunate and honored to be part. These royal premieres were always a high spot in counterpoint to all the hard work that was part of every Bond opening in London town.

*   *   *

Licence to Kill was very interesting from the get-go. Briefly titled *Licence Revoked*, it was soon changed but there continued much consternation at UA over whether the first word was to be spelled in the English style with a "C" or the American with an "S." After much "to-ing and fro-ing" the obvious transpired and the word appeared on the screen and in advertising as it was properly spelled in Bond's country. At first, we considered spelling in "American English" in the U.S. market, but the English press had spelled it with a "C" and a couple of weeks into production the "C" stuck. That ended any confusion. I was reminded of the earlier days of Bond when a solution to a minor billing problem was easily settled by having Cubby's name, as one of two equal producers, being placed first in the Western Hemisphere, and Harry's first in the Eastern. As someone once remarked, "The really big problems I can handle, it's the small ones that drive me nuts."

On location in Key West with fellow publicity executive Saul Cooper (standing) during *Licence to Kill*, 1988 (*Licence to Kill* © 1989 Danjaq, LLC, and Metro-Goldwyn-Mayer Studios Inc. All Rights Reserved).

Two or three weeks in Key West, Florida, was not a bad way to start any production, and I can't remember when a local government was more cooperative and helpful. However, Churubusco Studio in Mexico City was both geographically and philosophically quite a long way from well-run Pinewood!

As I worked my way through countless films over the years, I observed ever so many actors at or very near the start of their careers. To know which ones will find fame and fortune is almost an impossibility. For example, one never noticed future Academy Award winner George Chakiris when he was just another principal dancer in *White Christmas* back at Paramount. However, in *Licence to Kill*, it was hard not to be aware of the young, brooding, dangerously good-looking henchman Dario, who had a few scenes of menace before being dispatched by Bond toward the end of the film in an oversized meat-grinder. His demise is really quite graphic and harrowing. The point is that Benicio Del Toro went on to become a highly respected international star and won a well-deserved Oscar for *Traffic*. Actually, it was the principal villain, played by Robert Davi, who we all thought would achieve such heady heights. While certainly enjoying a most successful career, Davi never became the next Humphrey Bogart, which so many thought would be his due. No question, big screen movie acting and stardom are a combined dish that relatively few are considered by the public to have mixed correctly. Sometimes one is a "name" ever so briefly as the candlelight of fame often flickers out as quickly as it is lit and at such a dizzying height. To close the analogy, film stardom is a dish that very rarely stays hot for long.

I was somewhat bemused getting to know Pedro Armendariz, Jr., in Mexico City. I so well remembered my last encounter with his late father in a London Street. Our female lead Carey Lowell was a very good actress and was always cooperative with Saul et al. What more could one ask for? She later married Richard Gere and deserved her happiness while it lasted.

The famed Las Vegas singer Wayne Newton was quite the personality and, to my knowledge, the only Bond performer to ever arrive and leave in his own private airplane. Speaking of singing, like his fellow Italian-American named Sinatra, Davi was a helluva good crooner and would have been a WOW back in the big band days.

* * *

Saul Cooper left to produce and former UA vet Maurice Segal and his PR-savvy wife, Claire, took the U.S. reins, to my relief. The United States, Australia, the Far East, wherever—Tim Dalton and I were there selling all things Bond. This close involvement and solidarity of effort went a long way towards establishing our relationship, both professionally and personally. An actor on tour promoting a film is out of his normal environment and comfort zone, so it is up to the one responsible for "everything" to see that all goes as smoothly and effortlessly as possible, achieving the max with a minimum of angst. This was what those hours, days, weeks, and months of learning one's trade from the earlier years made possible. A position of responsibility and trust. One didn't just come into work from off the street for an Albert R. Broccoli.

Bond Postscript and Coda

First and foremost, I left EON in the best of hands by recommending UIP's Anne Bennett to be my successor. It was one of my best moves ever for the company. One day soon after retiring, I received a call to see if I was free to handle Tim Dalton's announcement that he had decided that two Bonds were enough and that he had other projects he wanted to do. I was flattered by the request and flew to South Carolina, where he was starring in a TV drama as Rhett Butler in a continuation of the *Gone with the Wind* story. All went well and it was great to be with Tim again and in less frenetic circumstances.

I also represented the company in Jamaica at a giant gathering of stars, press, and 007 aficionados, sponsored by the Ian Fleming Foundation and the Jamaica Tourist Board under the guidance of my good friend and the king of Bond memorabilia, Doug Redenius. It was actually fun to be a participant rather than an organizer for once, and what a pleasure it was seeing again old acquaintances like Maud Adams, Ursula Andress, Richard Kiel, and Grace Jones, plus meeting for the first time George Lazenby. I was also

Passing the baton: with my successor, senior UIP publicity executive Anne Bennett, at my retirement party at the RAF Hendon Museum, 1990. Beloved Bond actor Desmond Lewellyn is far left, to his right is Geoff Freeman, Saul Cooper and photographer Douglas Whitaker (©Danjaq, LLC).

With Eon's Dougie Noakes (left) and associate producer Tom Pevsner (center) at my retirement party, 1990 (©Danjaq, LLC).

pleased to meet again Jay Milligan, who owned and drove the car that spectacularly made the 360-degree jump over the river in *Golden Gun*, yet another of the many now gone, all missed, but remembered. The most magical moment for me, however, was briefly sitting at Ian Fleming's desk in his old villa, Goldeneye, where he wrote his 007 adventures.

At another such gathering at Stoke Poges near Pinewood and the site of the golf sequence in *Goldfinger* I met Lazenby again. This time he was newly married to the American tennis star Pam Shriver. She was very personable and friendly, but I'm sorry to say their "match" only lasted one set. This latter celebration put on by Doug Redenius of the Ian Fleming Foundation was also my last time to be with Desmond Llewelyn, who was soon after tragically killed in an auto accident near his Sussex home. He was a giant for us on so many of the promotional tours, and I feel very fortunate to have known him so well and to have been with him so often. He was most certainly a true, gentle man.

Over the retirement years I have enjoyed occasional visits to Bond sets at Pinewood and particularly in meeting with the new members of the fraternity. I was most impressed by Judi Dench and noted that she didn't give any indication of self-importance or of being impressed by her status as the grande dame of British acting. It was always good to see Pierce from time to time and he was as gracious as ever. Our conversations invariably centered on the early days.

Christopher Lee and his wife Gitte have remained friends and I was very pleased when he invited me down to the studio in Alicante when he filmed in Spain with

With Bond author and novelist Raymond Benson (left), Jamaica, 1996 (author's collection).

Penelope Cruz and the fine Irish actor Colin Farrell. I chatted at length with Farrell and he seemed genuinely interested in talking about the Bond days. I must say I found him to be very polite and correct. A genuine Irish "boyo" however. I was deeply moved by Lee's death and communicated by feelings to Gitte.

"We're with Jerry." With my friends and collaborators on this book, Mark Cerulli (left) and Doug Redenius (right), near Valencia, Spain, 2016 (author's collection).

Being invited up to London to the premieres have always been something to look forward to every couple of years, and none have been more exciting than the one at the Albert Hall. I believe *Skyfall* is one of the best Bonds ever and that Daniel Craig has been completely successful in making the role his own. Michael Wilson and Barbara Broccoli showed great wisdom in agreeing to Craig's original suggestion for a great talent like Sam Mendes to take the director's chair, and they equally showed much fortitude in knowing that the "control" factor of how the film would be conceived and executed was inevitably to involve much conversation, compromise, and acceptance by all in having to combine old and new elements in such a way as to come up with a mix that would be a credit to all concerned. The universal reviews of acclaim reflected on the success of their endeavors. *SPECTRE* has been the icing on the cake. The cut-free opening sequence in Mexico City is sheer brilliance.

As someone who knew them from Bond's very start, if and when I might ever encounter Cubby and Dana again, I will be very happy to pass on the word that their wonderful golden goose is in the safest of hands.

With longtime Bond enthusiast, writer/producer Mark Cerulli (right), before the *SPECTRE* premiere, London, 2015 (Cerulli collection, *SPECTRE* © 2015 Danjaq, LLC, Metro- Goldwyn-Mayer Studios Inc. and Columbia Pictures Industries, Inc. All Rights Reserved).

There have been countless millions of pages of words written about 007 and his world, but in all those books, magazines, and newspapers, not even one sentence has ever emerged, to the best of my knowledge, relating to what follows. It finishes my own account of this most remarkable enterprise and my part in its place in the history of motion picture entertainment.

In late summer 1962, Cubby and Harry decided to have a sneak preview of *Dr. No* in order to have a firsthand audience reaction. This was common practice in California but a rarity among filmmakers in Europe. Amidst great secrecy, the showing of "A Recently Completed Major Film" was duly advertised in the outer lobby and on the marquee of the Odeon Kensington cinema in West London. The theater was packed that night and a very nervous director, Terence Young, stood in the aisle behind the last row of the stalls along with Cubby, Harry, a couple of sound and camera technicians from Pinewood, along with Bud Ornstein and me representing United Artists. I half expected to see Ian Fleming, but if he was there I certainly never saw him.

Normally, the makers go out for a bite and a drink during the early part of such a showing, but we were all riveted from the opening frame. The laughter, the applause, the literal whoops and hollering was a happening of sheer wonder for all of us. Of course, no one there that night realized that we were watching cinema history. It was more than enough that the reaction cards were by a large majority—OUTSTANDING! The couple of thousand in the audience didn't know it, but they were to be the first of well over a billion of the world's population who followed that first handful in experiencing the adventures of the oh-so-special, special agent known as Double-O Seven. I am certain many of that mostly youthful crowd are still around to say, "I was there," but from those of us from EON/UA, I believe I am the only one still standing who can finally put in place the very last untold piece of the jigsaw that is the saga of James Bond.

Memorable Moments
Along the Way

Many years ago, Woody Allen made a fantasy film titled *Zelig*. It was about a rather nondescript nobody who was present at almost every major happening of the 20th century. While I have no such pretention of any involvement with earth-shattering events, I do feel my interactions with people of different levels of fame and/or celebrity has been singularly unique and wide-ranging. I am most certainly to be classified as an equal opportunity name-dropper. My career choice led to most of these encounters, but many can be chalked-up to nothing more than that phenomenon known as "the fickle finger of fate."

The following, from what I will rather facetiously call my Book of Golden Memories, is listed in no particular order of chronology or importance.

* * *

My father had sold a check-writer at a favorable price to a famous bakery in San Francisco's very large North Beach Italian community, so the owner invited him to visit Funston Field, near the Presidio, to watch his sponsored sandlot league baseball team. At that time its star player was probably better known because of his elder brother, Vince, who played in the outfield for San Francisco's minor league team, the Seals. When a little boy meets a ball player (even a sandlot level one), he is impressed only by his size and the aura of his uniform; but all my adult life I recalled with pride and awe meeting Joe DiMaggio at the very start of his storied career. To think that one day I would work in London, England, for a woman he married is a "bridge too far" in anyone's life of amazing coincidences.

* * *

For Paramount's opening of *The Girl Rush*, I devised a nationwide contest of a "Girls Rush to Hollywood," with twelve winners being flown to Southern California to visit the studio, lunch with star Rosalind Russell and others from the film, attend a private screening, and as the *piece de resistance*, be given a screen test. Ros said it was one of the best promotional ideas in which she was involved in a career spanning three decades. I personally selected from many thousands of photos sent in from every corner of the States twelve most attractive women from twelve different big cities across the country. Major local newspapers were made part of the promotion, so publicity galore!

One of the selected dozen was a very beautiful blonde from the New York area, whose name I unfortunately cannot recall, who was easily the most patrician of our lovelies in manner and background. The press attention changed her life even though she would have made it anyway. It wasn't too long before she was dating Ted Williams, one of baseball's greatest players of all time, who had recently divorced his first wife. One day I received a small box in the mail. It contained a then rare Boston Red Sox baseball cap with an unsigned card, but with one beautifully scripted word in a feminine hand—"Thanks."

* * *

We were in the middle of selling one of Bing Crosby's many films and I had to go up to nearby Del Mar's race track to meet with Bing, as he was there working with the trainer of his string of thoroughbred race horses. My assignment was to finalize details of an upcoming promotional schedule. When we were finished with business it was after lunch; he asked if I wanted to stay and watch a couple of races before driving back down to the studio. So, there I was alone with Bing in his finish-line box feeling very full of myself, when up came two men in linen suits and Panama hats to greet him. That is how I came to be introduced to one of the most controversial figures in modern American history, the fabled FBI chief, J. Edgar Hoover.

Amusingly, while having a drink with Bing in one of the many track bars before leaving, I was introduced to one of the two most infamous mobsters in Southern California, Mickey Cohen. I met another, Bugsy Siegel, in Vegas at his Flamingo Hotel about six months before he got his ticket punched.

* * *

A classmate of mine at military school was one of the star athletes during my years there. His name was John North and he later had a great success at football in college. He eventually went into coaching and became an assistant with the storied Green Bay Packers. When they came out to San Francisco to play the Forty-Niners at Keyzar Stadium in their very first year as a professional football team, John called me and I was able to watch the game standing behind the Packers' bench. This led to my being field side at another game with the Los Angeles Rams, where I met Pete Rozelle, then a lowly publicity writer for that franchise. I saw Rozelle from time to time after I went to Paramount in Hollywood, and when Pete became more senior in the Rams organization he asked me if I wanted to go to work for him. I was flattered but told him I was by then firmly committed to a life in the motion picture industry. I declined but with everlasting appreciation for the offer. I always wondered what would have happened to my life if I had hooked up with Rozelle in his early days. His storied career as the all-powerful commissioner of the National Football League is well documented, and who knows what would have happened for me if I had been right there, hanging on to his coattails for dear life from the start of his remarkable career? That was certainly the one time when I didn't take the fork in the road but remained on my determined path—for better or for worse.

*   *   *

At Fort Benning in Georgia, I was one of a select group invited to the officers club one day to hear a harp recital given by the Marx Brother called Harpo. Of course, he was famous for never uttering one word while in character, so the real charge was to be introduced and to hear him speak. He was a mesmerizing presence, and that afternoon it was his fans that were struck mute.

*   *   *

Staying in the nearby Georgia town of Columbus was the famous Hollywood buxom beauty Jane Russell. She was the wife of the great All-American football player Bob Warfield, who was also a second lieutenant at Fort Benning going through the same training as the rest of us ROTC types. One night I met them at an officers club dance and remember thinking, "Gee, they're just like everybody else." Naivety is wonderful when it doesn't get in the way of making a living.

*   *   *

When my wife and I had a villa in the south of Spain, we lived very near the tennis center in the Mijas-Coin area owned by Lew Hoad and his wife, Jenny. She had been a star player for Australia while Lew was one of its greatest men's champions of all time. They were great to know and be around, and

I always rejoiced at holding my own against Lew in many a table tennis encounter after a brew-fueled lunch. Hoad was a true Aussie, born and bred.

* * *

When briefly stationed at Camp Kilmer in New Jersey before shipping overseas, I met another army officer who was part of the permanent cadre at the camp. He had achieved fame on the New York stage and in a couple of films, most notably *Of Mice and Men*. His name—Burgess Meredith. He was very self-effacing and laid-back, just another junior officer with none of the "difficult" qualities which I was to later identify with so many of his fellow thespians. Years later I enjoyed his role as the elderly manager/trainer in the *Rocky* series. Of course, all of us in the services were guaranteed work "for the duration" and the universal disease common to most actors—"will I ever be offered another job after this one?"—didn't apply. This uncertainty was in an actor's makeup box, whether treading the boards of some theater or on a film set trying to make sure he was positioned so that the camera captured his "good side." Small wonder most were difficult; it is not a profession for the timid, no doubt about it.

* * *

Another "ships that pass in the night" occurrence with the famous took place in New York soon after my separation from the service. I was attending a Broadway show, and in the men's room during the interval I found myself at the urinals with Irving Berlin and Milton Berle alongside. The furthest thought from my mind was that one day I would come to know them both and to never have the nerve to tell either of that long-before initial brief encounter when each of us was busy holding onto his respective penis.

* * *

While working around films in production, one got to know many who were known as "working actors"—very professional men and women who came to the set, did their thing, and went home with a minimum of fuss and bother. All very nice to the little folk (like people in publicity). I must mention but a few of the many who were always a pleasure: Lloyd Nolan, Martin Balsam (father-in-law for a short time of one George Clooney), and Dean Jagger, with Desmond Llewelyn and Bernard Lee in the UK. Balsam will forever be famous as the ill-fated private eye in Hitch's *Psycho*.

On the distaff side, I must single out Thelma Ritter, the complete antithe-

187

sis of her usual wisecracking sardonic and cynical characterizations. This multiple Academy Award nominee (sadly, never a winner) was one of the most likable actors I ever knew and was always a real lady.

One of the few big stars who was a "working actor" in spirit and mentality was Peter Ustinov. A wit, raconteur, and talent of magic proportions.

* * *

The Hotel Raphael just off the Arc de Triomphe in Paris will always hold special memories for the few weeks I stayed there in a room sandwiched between the large suites of Ingrid Bergman and her then young brood on one side, and Darryl F. Zanuck and his latest French "discovery" on the other. Many a sleepless night was spent to the sounds of screaming children at play or screaming adults at whatever. The hotel's supposedly soundproof walls were not enough to muffle the din and maybe that was the downside for having been given that particular room at a special rate. The upside was always being greeted with a big smile and a courteous *"Bonjour Monsieur"* each and every time I met the very young and beautiful Isabella Rossellini in the hall.

* * *

In the summer of 1961 my wife and I briefly rented a house in the Hollywood hills just above famed Ciro's. It was owned by a well-known British pair, Margaret Leighton and her husband, Michael Wilding. Both were so laid back as to be almost horizontal. No lease, no specific routine for monthly payment, and no kind of the usual and normal security arrangements and/or guarantees. Leighton had met Lynn at Elstree Studios in England and, though not really knowing her, that was enough to be trusting. Naturally we bent over backwards in being correct toward them during our stay. Two comments—one was the photos and bits and pieces around the house relating to Wilding's former wife, Elizabeth Taylor, plus personal items left in closets and shelves by previous residents (friends mostly) like Sir Terence Rattigan and Anthony Newley. Their neighbor was no less a persona than Liberace, and he couldn't have been friendlier. I will long remember the night of the first moon landing, when we were all out in the street gazing up at the moon in the wonder of it all. Lee was jumping around liked a possessed schoolboy, totally caught up in the excitement of the historic moment.

* * *

During another stay in California in the late sixties, the murderous Manson gang struck and caused it to be a time of fear and craziness. The point of mentioning this is because about five days prior to the first killings, a group of us had been to the Academy Theater in Beverly Hills for a screening and went to the drugstore situated at the corner of the Beverly Wilshire Hotel for a light supper afterwards. In one of the booths was Roman Polanski's very pregnant wife, Sharon Tate, and a group of friends. I really don't know if any of those others were among the victims, but it was bad enough knowing that I was so near the ill-fated Tate only a few days prior to the bloodbath that took her life, some of her friends, and even that of her unborn child.

* * *

Donald Factor, the son of Max, the fabled King of Hollywood makeup, and his beautiful English partner became good friends and they invited us to stay with them. They lived on the beach at Malibu, probably the costliest stretch of sand in the whole world. While the houses were rustic and purpose-built for the sea and salt environment, it was the ocean view and the prime beach location, just to the north of Santa Monica, that made it the most desirable and exclusive place to live in all of Southern California. We got to know Donald's near neighbors, who included Larry Hagman and Julie Andrews with husband Blake Edwards. There were constant parties with the very rich and famous. What a way to go!

* * *

One day Lynn and I were in a ladies clothes shop in Beverly Hills when who walks in but Charles Bronson and his wife, the lovely English actress Jill Ireland. She and Lynn had been schoolchildren together back in the UK. It was

With Lynn, my beautiful wife of 44 years (photograph by Michael G. Wilson, author's collection).

quite a reunion, and Bronson was interested until he found I was not in a position to offer a starring role in any big movie. This more or less ended what would have been a nice renewal of the friendship for the two English roses so far from home. If I sound harsh about Bronson, please know that he was only doing what came naturally to many in the film industry. There was nothing personal, it was just a case of it being the way it was.

* * *

I well remember a big party at Arthur Jacob's beautiful home just off Sunset Boulevard with names galore: Natalie Wood, hubby Robert Wagner, Charlton Heston, Roddy McDowall, and Shirley Jones, to mention but five of ever so many. A typical Beverly Hills gathering of those fortunate few whom the gods saw fit to sprinkle with that extremely rare commodity—stardust! As I had not yet produced anything and was no longer a film company executive (just another senior employee of APJAC), so I was way down on the "What Can You Do For Me Today?" pecking order. I might as well not even have been there except for the short time Chuck Heston and I reminisced. I had to be content with my wife's beauty being the magnet for attention as far as the Juroe family was concerned.

A segue from these regular Jacobs star gatherings is to relate what happened to Arthur's wife after his sudden death from a massive heart attack. From being a much sought-after friend, Natalie was suddenly no longer the spouse of the "Great Producer," and there's not a lot a widow can do for an actor or actress employment-wise. She still had her real friends, but literally overnight, no longer the majority of the "reel" ones and it almost destroyed her. Natalie later married an Italian salesman for Gucci before her early death. She deserved better. It was right out of a Jackie Collins Hollywood novel.

* * *

Speaking of Jackie Collins, I met her when I was in London and regularly playing poker with a movie-related group at homes around Mayfair. She was at a couple of these gatherings with David Niven, Jr., who was as handsome as his father, although with no desire to be an actor. Her sister, Joan Collins, was lunching with Roger Moore and me at the Elephant Blanc on Curzon Street. It was great restaurant and "the local" to those of us who were working around the corner at EON. This was in the mid-eighties and I remember thinking: Gosh, our combined ages added up close to two hundred! Time is a difficult companion—but it sure beats the alternative! Obviously, I voiced no such thoughts to my very famous luncheon partners. It surely would have put them off their smoked salmon and scrambled eggs.

*   *   *

I was in the small shop in the lobby of the Castellana Hilton in Madrid looking for that day's *Herald Tribune* when a female voice boomed, "Juroe, you little shit, what are you doing here?" It was dear Ava Gardner. She always had a military way of usually calling most male acquaintances (from work) by their last name. As for the descriptive, Ava was always rural North Carolina born and bred, and to her credit never ever pretended being anything else. Most who knew her well adored her, as she was truly a one-off. Not many women ever lived a life with the mentality of a man yet remained so feminine. Of course, being one of the most beautiful females of all time didn't hurt! Be that as it may, most "feminists" might aspire to be what Ava was in living her life but, sadly, very few will ever come close.

*   *   *

Over the years, I came to meet two surgeons of much renown. One was Dr. Christiaan Barnard, the great heart specialist from South Africa. We were both guests at the same intimate dinner party given by one of Rio's top socialites when I was there on one of my distribution trips. The other one was in New York when I was briefly a near neighbor of Dr. Ramon Castro-viejo, the Spanish *émigré* then considered to be the greatest eye surgeon ever. His brilliant innovative work was long before the laser was even a gleam in some inventor's eye. Sorry!

*   *   *

Also, while in New York that summer of 1961, through the invites of a mutual friend, I was at many parties and dinners with the weird and wonderful Catalan painter, Salvador Dali. His eccentricity of manner and dress was every bit as evident as his genius at the easel. An unforgettable character in every sense.

In Paris in the fifties, I had occasion to visit the ateliers of Picasso and Fujita. To meet these great artists where they worked was humbling to say the least.

*   *   *

It was at a big gathering at Shirley MacLaine's invitation that I met Bobby Kennedy shortly after he announced his candidacy for president. Finally, it became my turn to have a few words with him and I must admit it was most disconcerting, as he was always looking over my shoulder as if searching the room for who knows what. Maybe I wasn't being interesting enough or just wasn't important enough, I don't know. It was certainly a disquieting minute or two and I was quite happy to converse with one of his acolytes when Shirley moved him on to yet another possible future voter. Perhaps being the only Republican in the room showed? I'll never know.

I met his brother Ted in Paris at a private dinner. He was there with the beautiful daughter of some European minister. The young U.S. senator was a very difficult person to be around and he made it obvious that the other six of us were like extras in a crowd scene, just there to make up the numbers. Very strange when it was quite well known by all that our host, a very wealthy American expat living in Paris, was the inamorata of Kennedy's "date." Why she was partnered with the latter for the evening for whatever reasons was none of our business!

I was introduced to Jackie Kennedy in Athens by Michael Cacoyannis when she was married to his good friend, Aristotle Onassis. It was quite something to even be in the same room with those two at that time. She couldn't have been more gracious in greeting yet another fawning stranger and had a great ability of making one feel she was genuinely pleased to meet you. I always felt her life should have been lived on a stage but with a happier final act.

While I was with Universal in New York there was a short-lived plan to have an Eastern version of its studio tour with props, cameras, lights, and the whole nine yards. The venue was to be a humongous warehouse complex in lower Manhattan. That is how I came to meet Caroline Kennedy Schlossberg as she and her husband were owners of the property. Unfortunately, the idea came to nothing, but it was certainly an interesting idea while it lasted.

* * *

While with Universal I regularly had to go to the studio for meetings, as the company's headquarters were there. On one of the trips I read in the trades (*Variety* and *The Hollywood Reporter*) that my old friend Bud Ornstein was out at Warner Bros. on business. I immediately called and learned that he and Gwynne were staying at Pickfair in Beverly Hills with her Aunt Mary. Would Lynn and I like to come to lunch there? To be invited to visit the most famous home in all Southern California was an extraordinary opportunity not to be missed, and I almost jumped down the phone line in agreeing.

Mock Tudor on the outside, Pickfair was baronial inside and its acres of grounds on top of one of the highest hills in all of western Los Angeles made for a humbling feeling as well as a truly spectacular 360-degree view. I am certain a commoner going to Balmoral for the first time would have the same feelings that I had at being in the fabulous home built by Hollywood's own royal pair—Douglas Fairbanks and Mary Pickford.

At a sit-down, rather formal lunch with service by very British servants wearing white gloves, was Mary's current husband, the very handsome Charles "Buddy" Rogers, always to be known as the star of the very first motion picture to win an Academy Award, *Wings* (for the 1927–28 ceremony). There was no sign of the lady of the house during the meal, and it was while we were having coffee that Bud asked if I would like to meet Mary. I responded, "Yes, please," and he led me to a small lift which only took the two of us up the one level. We walked down a beautifully carpeted hall to a pair of highly polished doors. Bud lightly knocked and called out, "Mary, it's Bud, I'm here with Jerry Juroe, whom I told you about."

We stood there a few moments and a voice on the other side of the door said, "Jerry, it's nice to meet you. I'm so glad you were able to visit, as Bud told me what a good friend you've been to him and to Gwynne."

I mumbled a few words in response and, after what seemed an eternity, the disembodied voice said, "Thank you so much for coming. I've enjoyed meeting you. Bye bye."

Bud took me by the elbow and we quietly made our way back to the lift. I had "met" Mary Pickford, the actress who was once the most famous woman on the planet and truly the first global movie star. It was one of the most unusual encounters with celebrity that one could possibly imagine.

* * *

Two offshoots of that visit took place back in London. One was at the very upmarket restaurant that was in the building next door to Bud and Gwynne's fabulous duplex apartment in the heart of Mayfair behind the Ritz Hotel. It was there that I met yet another founder of United Artists when Charlie Chaplin came over to Bud's table to say hello to Gwynne, whom he had known from babyhood (hers).

Through Bud I was asked to help in the organization of a big American/British World War II remembrance activity led by Douglas Fairbanks, Jr. He was as sophisticated as it was possible for a "yank" to be, and he was the perfect example of the urbane and polished upper-class Anglophile.

It was a pleasure to be briefly involved in a project with this most distinguished American. He was the only one I ever talked with about my father's naval service as an officer in both world wars. Perhaps that was due to Doug's fine record as a U.S. naval commander in the Second World War. Quite separately, it was bemusing to meet another with the "Junior" appellation, though his surname was slightly more patrician—to state the obvious.

* * *

There was a marvelous expression in the military to describe when someone of a senior position would take advantage of a situation by making crystal clear to one and all that he was speaking from a level of great authority and importance. It was called "pulling rank," and the expression perfectly captures the actions of the actor Glenn Ford during the making of *Love Is a Ball* at the Victorine Studios in Nice in the south of France. In Leo Fuchs we had possibly the very best special photographer in Europe assigned to cover the film. He was not only extremely competent in taking clever pictures, but most importantly had a great record in having his work published in top periodicals around the world.

For some reason Ford became very agitated because co-star Hope Lange really seemed to enjoy the attention of Leo behind his lens. To the great chagrin of producer Marty Poll, we had to take Leo off the assignment. Of course, he went with full pay, charged against the picture. Also, some surefire publicity went down the drain with Fuch's departure. When the star of a film was the most important element in a production being financed, then he (or she) wields great power during the making of that film. This is what happened on *Love Is a Ball*, and I am pleased, even after all those years, to still be around to set the record straight on at least one experience of frustration among the many examples of the often-times cavalier treatment of people who were just in there trying to do their jobs. I don't mean to single out one particular personality in recounting this example of injustice, but it is typical of what can happen that could drive one absolutely bonkers. The other side of the coin in *Love Is a Ball* was the veteran Charles Boyer, a perfect example of what a movie star was all about.

* * *

An American actor away from his comfort zone can suddenly feel exposed and vulnerable when out and about, particularly if in a foreign locale. He is suddenly very content to be joined by a compatriot in (1) language, (2) nationality, and (3) industry. I particularly remember a breakfast with the fine New York actor Harvey Keitel at the Four Seasons Hotel in Munich, Germany, and a supper in the bar of the Hôtel de Crillon in Paris with the charming Patrick Swayze. These sudden invites to join a lonely diner in a foreign clime illustrate the phenomenon of but one facet of what constitutes social interaction between stars and those who populate lower echelons of the motion picture industry. All it takes is a warm, "Hello," the use of a first name, and an ease of manner that indicates you are a compatriot in the business, and *voila!* You're quickly accepted as a long-lost friend, although you are complete and total strangers.

*   *   *

I would be remiss not to mention the two famed army generals I came to know. One was commander of all U.S. forces in the western part of the United States. Based at the Presidio in San Francisco following the Korean War, four-star General Mark Clark made it very clear to a subordinate (everyone!) that one was in the presence of greatness. The other was the polar opposite in demeanor—General Norman Schwarzkopf was a pleasure. He and his gracious wife lived across a small lake from us in the estates section of the Cheval Golf Club in the upper reaches of Tampa, Florida. This was in the early nineties after his great achievement as supreme commander during the first Gulf War when he brilliantly led the liberation of Kuwait. He was as gracious and warm in personality as he was large in girth. I know for a fact that he was constantly rejecting entreaties to become political and run for high office. I am convinced that as a boy he was aware of all the sniping and vitriol that his father (then head of the New Jersey State Police) received in the 1930s following his part in the capture, conviction and subsequent execution of Bruno Hoffman for the kidnap/murder of the infant son of Charles Lindbergh, America's greatest hero at the time. To be exposed to the vacillations of a media mired in its Hearst-like obsession with the selling of newsprint instead of facts is not for everyone! I've known great British showbiz journalists, people like Donald Zec, Bill Hall, Peter Evans, Mike Davies, and Roderick Mann. They were always fair and honest in what they wrote and I respected them all. Of course, if one was in the public eye, then having to cope with any media bias was always a possibility.

As late as the eighties, most people still thought "spin" was something done by a propeller.

*   *   *

My most recent brush with the "anointed few" was at the 65th anniversary of the Normandy landings. As one of some hundred veterans of the beaches sitting behind the world leaders as they spoke on the podium at the great Omaha Beach Cemetery it was my fate, yet again, to be in the right place at the right time. I was in an aisle seat, toward the rear of our gathering, and when the leaders lined up for the wreath laying ceremony at the back of the esplanade they were standing right next to my chair. My photo records this historic moment. Afterwards we actually had the opportunity to interact with the dignitaries, HRH Prince Charles, Presidents Obama and Sarkozy, as well as the British and Canadian prime ministers in a scrum that must have driven those charged with security somewhat crazy. Though not my cup of tea politically, I still felt most honored to actually meet and speak to my country's commander-in-chief. A heady moment to be sure.

In that hectic milling crowd of mostly Americans, I noticed a somewhat bemused Prince Charles standing nearby. Not the absolute center of the universe for once, he was looking at me as if to say, "Is that American possibly someone I've met before?" I went to him and said, "Sir, it's certainly a bit different from our past meetings to do with James Bond." The penny dropped and his smile of recognition with someone he could speak to, if only for a passing minute, was as heartwarming as it was genuine. One of my finer moments.

* * *

In San Francisco, during the filming of *A View to a Kill*, there was a meeting at City Hall with its lady mayor. What a gracious person was (now Senator) Diane Feinstein, a perfect example of why there should never be something called "a glass ceiling."

* * *

In the heart of London on Jermyn Street was one of the most exclusive men's Turkish baths in all the world. It was there one afternoon in the early seventies that I met the great American singer, Tony Martin. He was at the top for over fifty years, and his warmth of personality reflected a man totally at ease with his status as a premiere entertainer. We became friends and, at his insistence, the next time I was in Southern California I had a delightful lunch at Tony's Beverly Hills home. His wife, the mesmerizing Cyd Charisse, was as striking in person as she was on stage or screen. "Imposing" doesn't begin to convey her persona. I felt honored to be with them in their home.

* * *

196

I met the great composer/conductor David Rose in Paris, and it was fascinating to be at a couple of meals with the man who wrote one of the biggest hits of the World War II era, "Holiday for Strings." The Glenn Miller Air Force Orchestra had played it at every concert while I was with them.

* * *

When I was with Paramount in London, there was a major corporate gathering of its personalities with a big gala dinner at the close. I sat at a table that included a couple of very interesting people. I had never met Christopher Plummer when he made *The Return of the Pink Panther* for UA nor on any of the films he made over a career that is amazing in its longevity. His list of credits is quite astonishing. He was a very erudite man and I regret not really knowing him. One of many major acting names who hailed from Canada, his close friendship with compatriot Oscar Peterson, one of the world's all-time great jazz pianists, says it all. Plummer was soon to marry his delightful dinner companion, actress Elaine Taylor, who was under contract to Paramount at the time. Theirs has been a long and successful union and it is somewhat amazing that such a major star has managed to remain "under the radar" of the tabloid media.

The other fellow diner was the tall rangy American James Coburn. He was great fun and quite the raconteur. If I were to sum him up in one word it would be "eccentric." His dinner companion was as short as he was tall, and was as pleasant as she was attractive—singer Lynsey de Paul was yet another of those who made one wonder why stardom overlooked so many who appeared to be deserving.

* * *

Hal Wallis was one of the all time great filmmakers. I never spent much time around him at Paramount in the fifties, although I became quite close to his head of publicity, Walter Seltzer, one of the best of our breed. Wallis was in Paris on a promotional tour with one of his many acting discoveries, Lizabeth Scott. My wife and I attended a private dinner with them at the home of Paramount's European head, John Nathan. To "break bread" with a person like Hal Wallis was something that would never have happened to me in Hollywood. He was one of the wealthiest in an industry well known for being at the top of the scale in terms of remuneration. Between them, Wallis and Bob Hope at one time owned a very large part of the San Fernando Valley.

* * *

I was in Berlin and had to contact Jimmy Stewart, who was there with his lovely wife, Gloria. It had not been too long since the death of her son in combat in Vietnam, and Stewart asked if I wanted to join them for lunch. He said he was trying to keep her occupied with fresh faces to talk about anything except the obvious. As it turned out, the entire time we were together we talked about World War II.

* * *

When I went to the UK in 1956 for Monroe, I rented a flat in Upper Brook Street, between Grosvenor Square and Park Lane. To me it was not expensive, as just my living allowance more than covered the rental. At this time £12 per week was the average salary in the UK, so I guess I was the 1950s version of the Yank who was "overpaid, oversexed, and over here." At first I didn't realize how "posh" the apartment and its location was. I'll never forget when I threw a small "going away party" for Esther Williams (charged to her company obviously!) when she finished her aquacade show. On entering she said, "My God, Jerry, you're living better than I am." Not true in my opinion, as her rented house near Regent's Park was super lux, but the immense standard of living divide between motion picture stars and the vast majority of show business humanity was blurred when away from a Beverly Hills or a New York City.

One of the others with a flat in the small four-story block was the scion to one of Britain's wealthiest shipping families. He had gone to all the right schools, was very upper class and was part of Princess Margaret's then inner circle. One day he asked if I wanted to join him at a small party with Her Royal Highness. Seems he had mentioned me and what I did and (most importantly) for whom, so I guess she wanted to know all the inside gen on my boss. In that summer and fall of 1956, Marilyn Monroe's name was an "Open Sesame" anywhere, anytime, anyplace! That is how I ended up enjoying cocktails and even having a dance at Les Ambassador's Club with the world's most famous little sister.

* * *

During the height of my interest and involvement with bullfighting, I got to know two major figures from Mexico's La Fiesta Brava. They were every bit the equal of movie stars in earning power and fan adulation in the Spanish-speaking world where the *corrida* was a way of life. One was the great Carlos Arruza, who was second in ranking only to Spain's immortal Manolete. The other was the mercurial Luis Procuna. Both were larger than life and, even from a masculine viewpoint, it was not too difficult to understand Ava Gardner's famous interest in those who were stars in the world of blood and sand.

*   *   *

When a group of us were on tour in Latin America for Bond, we duly went to Buenos Aires. At the time one of our principal Bond Girls was the former Miss World from Sweden, Mary Stavin. Mary was well known then as being the partner of Northern Ireland's George Best, one of the world's greatest soccer players, so that was enough of a connection for the gregarious Argentine football "god" Maradona to be with us from arrival until we left three days later. Even a tenuous connection like that is enough for that very rare and exclusive Club of Celebrity to come into play. I guess there is no question that too much fame comes hand-in-glove with a very special kind of mink-lined loneliness and caution in interaction with others.

Finding "equals" in fame when they are so few and far between is obviously not an easy thing. I guess it's the dark side of the mirror that reflects the glory that is on the surface.

*   *   *

Sharing a laugh with former Miss World Mary Stavin at a post-premiere dinner for *Octopussy*, 1983 (UIP, *Octopussy* © 1983 Danjaq, LLC, and Metro-Goldwyn-Mayer Studios Inc. All Rights Reserved).

One day there was a big luncheon gathering at Pinewood of many of the names who filmed there over the years. In the restaurant, I was suddenly in conversation with Ernie Wise. What a delight he was to meet. His career had totally changed since, tragically, he was no longer part of the most successful comedy double act in the world. Anyway, I thoroughly enjoyed meeting him and talking about my time with Hope. Monroe's name received the usual flicker of interest, but it was my unique recollections of Bob that captured his interest. A refreshing change.

The short Mr. Wise leads me to comment on an observation rarely mentioned. Leading men are always thought to be the proverbial tall, dark, and handsome up there on the screen. Not so. Some were eye-to-eye with me at barely five-foot-eight or just an inch or two taller at most. Exactly as in normal life, some handled it better than others. Among those I worked with, or met, this vertically challenged group included Alan Ladd, Richard Gere, Montgomery Clift, Tom Cruise, Dustin Hoffman, Al Pacino, and the tallest of this small lot, Albert Finney. They all achieved major stardom, and each is to be lauded in overcoming a shared "problem." One has to accept having to play the hand you're dealt. As Sinatra's song went, "That's Life."

* * *

I still have a Romanoff's Restaurant ashtray on my desk as I write this. I was in the iconic Beverly Hills eatery with Gloria Grahame for lunch during her publicity activity for *The Greatest Show on Earth*. Romanoff himself came to our booth to greet her and give a small commemorative gift of a boxed ashtray. I got one, too, for merely being there, I guess. Just sitting at a table anywhere having a private lunch with Gloria was the stuff that dreams are made of.

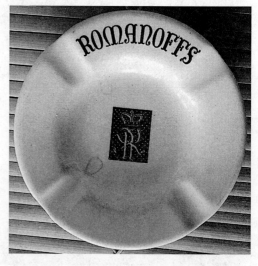

As scarce as hen's teeth: an ashtray from Romanoff's, the exclusive Beverly Hills restaurant, given to Gloria Grahame and me by Romanoff himself (author's collection).

* * *

The restaurant/bar in the Sherry-Netherland in New York was the setting for an unforgettable St. Patrick's Day with the great star Jack Lemmon. I was with Universal and he was promoting his latest film. We were supposed to have a couple of newspaper interviews elsewhere, but Jack became quite content to stay at our hotel. While the parade and the crowds were outside, we were ensconced in a most salubrious mink-lined setting for the day. Jack handled each journalist like the pro he was and surprisingly was as *compos mentis* in the late afternoon as he was hours before when we started. The bar bill might have soared, but Lemmon remained on an even keel with astonishing grace and poise.

Every single one of the countless fans who endlessly showed up at our large booth to ask for a photo or just to say hello was treated with the same courtesy and appreciation by Lemmon. He was a master of what was required of a true star when out in the public eye. This jovial and gregarious actor was the American equal of Roger Moore in dealing with both the public and the press. That is some compliment as far as I'm concerned.

*   *   *

When I was first in Hollywood and on my own, I tried to have dinner every couple of weeks at the famed Brown Derby on Vine Street, just down from Hollywood Boulevard. Over a period of time I often found myself in adjoining booths to two very different stars who were also there almost always eating alone. Though miles apart in name recognition and their respective places on the rungs of stardom, John Payne and Bette Davis were alike in nodding a greeting of recognition after a while. There was never a conversation, just a tilt of the head—but for a young newcomer to the fame game, it was more than enough.

*   *   *

When I was in New York I often visited a good friend who lived in Sutton Place, by the river on the East Side. I was always on the lookout for Greta Garbo, who lived in the adjoining apartment building, but never saw her once. However, I only had to leave the Universal offices and walk across 55th Street to the Akbar Restaurant for an Indian meal to see, with amazing regularity, the once great star Paulette Goddard, who lived in splendor high in the skyscraper above the eatery. One day I was introduced by a showbiz journalist who knew her, and after that meeting I would always say "Hello, Miss Goddard," in passing and get a warm response each and every time. She was no longer the great beauty of her earlier Paramount heyday, but she still was accustomed to being recognized and was seemingly quite content with a most enviable way of life out of the limelight that had gone before. She was little more than a teenager when discovered by Charlie Chaplin, no less. She supposedly had one of the largest private collections of jewelry and was most certainly the Elizabeth Taylor of her day. I always wanted to ask her if she wanted to join me in the restaurant for a drink, but never had the nerve.

* * *

In London in the seventies, I was in a restaurant in Mayfair with my wife and friends when who walked in but Bing Crosby. He saw me, walked up to the table, held out his hand in greeting, and said, "Hi, Jerry, how are you?" It was one of my most surprising moments. Movie performers usually didn't remember your name two weeks after last working together, yet here was one of the truly greatest stars remembering someone by name after some ten years! Maybe that was part of what made Bing the well-loved personality and world figure that he was. To say that I was "chuffed" is one of the understatements of all time.

* * *

We were having dinner at a famous Paris brasserie and a couple of tables down against the opposite wall were the archetypical movie mogul, Darryl F. Zanuck, and Irina Demick, from his megahit, *The Longest Day*. Naturally there was no recognition from him, although I certainly had been around him at studios and hotels often enough. All was normal until, with coffee, I pulled out a large Churchill-size Cuban cigar (those were the days!) and duly lit up. My Havana more than matched his in girth and length and that's all it took for a reaction from the Great Producer. When leaving, as he was walking out, he came across to our table and said, in passing, "How's it going?" In a million years that would never have happened if I hadn't been a fellow smoker with such an imposing cigar. I was a member of some exclusive and rarified fraternity without even knowing it, and for once in my life I proved that size *was* everything!

* * *

Roger Moore and I were having breakfast in the coffee shop at a Tokyo Hotel when who walked in but George Hamilton with a good friend and PR colleague of mine, Enrique Herreros from Madrid. They were also in Japan to promote a movie, and it was most pleasant for all of us to meet up so unexpectedly. Suddenly, the manager appeared. Having a very limited English capability, he pointed to his camera and gesticulated—was it all right to take a picture? I motioned that it was okay, and he took a couple. Bowing "thanks" as only a Japanese can, he moved off. A couple of minutes passed and he returned, motioning for me to join him at another table. He then handed me paper and pen and mimed writing down names, obviously for a left-to-right identification, so I wrote out "Kiki's" name and mine. He then indicated that he wanted the names of the other two—meaning Messrs. Moore and Hamilton. I did so and, breaking up with laughter, rejoined our two world famous stars. When I told them what happened, they did see the funny side, but certainly not to the degree of the two "equally unknown" publicists in the group!

* * *

While in Paris, my job obviously put me in contact with the world-acclaimed newspaper columnist Art Buchwald. He was as nice a man as his humorous writings indicated him to be and over time we came to know each other quite well. Through Art, I met two very famous American novelists, one living on the most exclusive island on the Seine in the center of Paris, and the other in semi-permanent residence on the Left Bank. There were many literary gatherings at their homes. Both James Jones of *From Here to Eternity* fame and the prolific Irwin Shaw threw some of the best "well-oiled" get-togethers since the halcyon days of Hemingway and Fitzgerald. It was humbling to be even a very small part of such a group in the Paris of the sixties.

* * *

An interesting interaction of stars took place in the bar of Rome's famed Hassler Hotel when I was there with Roger Moore during one of our many Grande Bond Tours. He had contacted Liza Minnelli, who was in Rome on holiday between singing appearances and invited her to join him for a lunch. I was with them and a couple of others prior to their going on to eat. A swarthy fellow with a very full Magnum-style mustache walked in and was immediately recognized as Harry Reems, the male star of the wildly successful porn film *Deep Throat*. Both Moore and Minnelli treated him as one of The Club and everyone there wanted to meet this (at that time) most controversial of actors. He was totally at ease—and why not, really? It became abundantly clear to me that day that pornographic movies had come a long way in the latter half of the 20th century. The breakthrough success of *Deep Throat* had made that genre firmly part of the mainstream of entertainment.

My only comment on this phenomenon is to question if the astronomical sale of pornographic videos and DVDs for home showing was the reason for the dramatic fall in sales of men's raincoats of seedy Soho fame.

*   *   *

On one of my many business trips to New York while with UA, I was told in advance to keep my first evening there open, as there were two house tickets in my name at the box office to see the giant Broadway hit show *Fiddler on the Roof* and to have a backstage visit to the dressing room of star Zero Mostel. At that time, everyone thought that he would play Tevya in UA's screen version, as the company had just acquired the film rights to much acclaim. Meeting Zero was joyful and we became quite close when he made *A Funny Thing Happened on the Way to the Forum* in Madrid a couple of years later. Anyway, the next day in the office, one of UA's top execs asked not the usual, "How did you like the show?" but rather the question was, "What was the audience reaction?"

I thought quickly and was quite proud of my answer and the response to it from those in the room. I simply said, "Half the audience was crying because they were Jewish and the other half because they weren't." A comment sure to melt the heart of the hardest New York film company executive. I might have been "one toy short of a piñata" in some ways, but I surely knew on which side my bagel was buttered. I was passing like some NFL Super Bowl quarterback, no two ways about it!

In Madrid for UA's *A Funny Thing Happened on the Way to the Forum* with Zero Mostel (right), 1966. UA's Fred Goldberg is to the left (UA/UIP Spain).

*   *   *

204

I had become friendly with director Budd Boetticher at Matador Carlos Arruza's Bull Ranch, so when I realized I was to be near the Mexican location of his new production, I called him. He invited me to stop by and have lunch. That was how I first met the stunning Maureen O'Hara. She was long gone from her heyday, but was still the (more mature) red-headed beauty of her prime in *The Quiet Man* in my eyes. In real life she spoke with more of an Irish lilt than when acting, but that only added to her allure.

* * *

A meeting at Dino de Laurentiis' office in Rome (before his Italian studio time) featured a half hour of equal pain and pleasure. Sitting in a large leather chair in front of his Mussolini-sized desk was wife Silvana Mangano. Ten years on from her steamy performance in *Bitter Rice*, she was still in her late twenties and every inch the equal of Sophia Loren, wife of Dino's partner, Carlo Ponti.

There I was in the matching chair opposite, trying desperately to pay attention to Dino and not be distracted by the silk stocking-displayed legs ending with black lace covering a sight that could have caused the fall of any Roman Empire, much less a young publicity peon just trying to do his job. As I finally stumbled out into the street, I could only hope that I had upheld the honor of Paramount. As for *la bella* Silvana, she probably didn't even know I was there. One could say she fiddled while I burned.

* * *

Another "unconscious flasher" of note was dear Esther Williams. Maybe she was so used to being seen in only a bathing suit, she didn't even think about it; but it was impossible to meet at her home without being given a show that featured her satin or silk-covered wares. She was truly a happy camper and her enthusiasm was never ending. She was the Duracell Bunny of performers. I really liked her.

* * *

My all time favorite location was for a film I never even worked on. Amazingly, Bond sites like the Topkapi Museum in Istanbul, the top of the rock of Gibraltar, or the Sugarloaf in Rio all pale for me when compared to the monolithic mountainous outcropping that is Hanging Rock, near Melbourne in Australia.

Every time I made a trip Down Under, I tried to arrange things so I had a free day in Melbourne so I could visit and revisit this magic mystery of a place. Peter Weir's *Picnic at Hanging Rock*, with its haunting and ravishing musical score played on the pipes of some enchanted Pan was quite simply one of my favorite films.

Welcome to the rock: at an eerie location from *Picnic at Hanging Rock*, one of my favorite films, near Melbourne, Australia. Photograph taken by none other than Timothy Dalton while on tour for *The Living Daylights* (author's collection, *The Living Daylights* © 1987 Danjaq, LLC, and Metro-Goldwyn-Mayer Studios Inc. All Rights Reserved).

I was last there with Timothy Dalton, and I treasure his photo of me at the exact spot where in the film the beautiful schoolgirl Miranda disappears as time stands still. London's *Evening Standard* put it best—"a film that provokes the mind long after it has seduced the senses."

* * *

The premiere of *Chariots of Fire* was a night to remember. The producer was Jack Weiner, who had been Columbia's top publicity honcho in Europe. We were good friends, and that is how I was there and at the post-picture party in the company of his fellow producer of their first (and only) film. This most pleasant young man would become world famous, but for all the wrong reasons. His name was Dodi Fayed.

* * *

Shirley MacLaine's co-star in *The Bliss of Mrs. Blossom* was the very easy-going James Booth. Everyone thought he would become a big star and, while a hit on stage in the West End, he never crossed that invisible line that said *star* on the screen. When *Zulu* was cast, it was assumed Booth, in the part of the somewhat cowardly "sick" soldier (who became one of the real-life heroes of the Battle at Rorke's Drift), would become the next *big thing*. Not to be. His character might win a Cross named Victoria in real life, but the relative unknown Michael Caine would go on to win a couple of statues named Oscar, not to mention worldwide fame and adulation.

* * *

As of this writing, there have been many actors with whom I have stayed in a countless number of hotel suites around the globe. My most unforgettable single moment with one of them is recounted with the actor unnamed. I opened the door to his bedroom expecting to find him ready to go to our next media appointment; I found him in what I can only describe as an embarrassing situation. What made it all so difficult was that the lady in question was our maid, who could easily have auditioned as one of Macbeth's three witches without need of makeup or wig. I mumbled a quick apology, closed the door, and beat a hasty retreat. For the next two days, I couldn't look our star in the face and not show my amusement at his ongoing discomfort. Finally, he couldn't stand it anymore and he just shouted, "She needed the money!"

* * *

When I was with Columbia in London, a film project was announced involving Muhammad Ali, and when he came to London for the pronouncement there, he was ensconced in a suite at the Savoy. I can truly say it was quite something to meet and have the opportunity to briefly chat with one of the world's truly iconic figures. I left both shaken and stirred, and with not a Pinewood martini in sight.

* * *

Brigitte Bardot owned a flat on the Left Bank's Rue de Bac, and I learned it was for sale prior to it being announced. She was making *Viva Maria* for UA at the time, so I quickly went out to the Boulogne studio to ask her what she wanted for it. This was followed by much haggling, via her Realtor. I finally gave up the idea, as every time I made an offer—below her inflated asking price—her response was a rise in the cost; so I finally threw in the towel. If she hadn't made it as an actress, Mademoiselle Bardot would have been a great distaff Donald Trump.

* * *

Small avant-garde jazz groups were prevalent in the San Francisco of the immediate post-war years, and the "hot ticket" was the Cuban rhythm of Joe Castro. He was even bigger at that time than another virtuoso jazz pianist, Dave Brubeck, who was also making a name for himself in the Bay Area clubs. I became friendly with them both, and through the very handsome and personable Castro, I came to know the lady he married, the storied heiress Doris Duke. As a result, Joe could not only afford a baby grand, but also the entire Steinway catalogue, if not the whole company.

* * *

While I was with Columbia in London, I had to go to Portsmouth for a special photo session at the navy yard with George Sanders. We returned by car to London and I found his "air of boredom" that was so much a part of his screen persona carried over to his reaction to his profession of movie actor. Of course, any man who married not one, but two Gabor sisters had to be just a bit different, and his suicide at only sixty-six reflected on his *ennui*, not only with his work, but life in general. A most unusual character to have met, if ever so briefly.

* * *

While I was in Paris, I was asked to collect a script directly from Omar Sharif in his hotel suite. It was evidently something so top secret that normal delivery methods were not to be trusted. I arrived, and to my surprise, was invited in and plied with food, drink, and conversation. Sharif and his beautiful young blonde companion treated me as some kind of longtime friend. Unusual behavior, but it seemed to be most sincere conduct on his part. I was reminded of a day years before in London, when I had to meet Otto Preminger at his hotel. Upon entering his palatial rooms, he introduced me to his lovely lady in residence with the unforgettable words, "Ah, Jerry, I don't believe you've met my mistress."

*   *   *

Though my time with Columbia was short, in time it seemed to be eventful nonetheless. While I was there, *Robin and Marian* was made, and I was sent to Switzerland to assist a somewhat frail Audrey Hepburn on her trip to the UK prior to filming. She was greatly changed, but I was pleased she remembered me from our Paramount days. For all the glamour and success, her life had not been a cakewalk. A perfect example of the peaks and valleys that are part of everyone's journey.

*   *   *

On my first trip to London after joining United Artists, I was in the office of longtime managing director, Monte Morton. At one point he asked if I would screen a film made by the son of dear friends of his. He wanted anyone at UA with a small degree of authority (me!) to give an objective reaction and thereby get him off the hook with his friends. It was obviously a piece of crap, as I was quick to discover. While interesting in concept, it was amateurish in a professional way. I cannot explain this ambiguous reaction any clearer than that. As I left the projection room, Morton immediately took me to lunch, where I had to explain to our very young wannabe director, one Michael Winner, that he might make a film one day for UA. He did, but *The Cool Mikado* wasn't it. It was all most uneasy, and I was practically apologizing for not considering his earliest cinematographic effort good enough.

The prolific American novelist and screenwriter Budd Schulberg had written a shocking story about film industry people titled *What Makes Sammy Run?* I realized that I had a real live Sammy before me, albeit a very English one. It wasn't my fault that the lead character of *The Cool Mikado* wasn't played by some yet unknown discovery named Charles Bronson. I never encountered

Winner again, but that first and only time was more than enough for me. I always felt he lived a life far more interesting than any of his many pictures.

*   *   *

Most actors have successful careers resulting from an ability to be believable playing characters wildly different in style and substance. There are others equally successful, who basically always play themselves no matter the demands of the script. Clark Gable, Gary Cooper, and John Wayne are prime examples of those who become King of the Mountain by just simply being themselves. Makeup, wardrobe, accent, whatever—it mattered not. As the cartoon character, Popeye, once said, "I am what I am!"

Then there are those few who become totally sublimated by a character that overwhelms their own identity. Two great instances of this latter type were actors I had to meet separately in Rome prior to each going off to a distant island or mountain location where press visits were of little concern to a producer whose only problem was finishing his film with a minimum of bother and interference. To be sitting at one of the pavement tables at Doney's on the Via Veneto with a world-famous actor and not once hearing him called by his real name is somewhat unnerving. However, neither Peter Falk nor Telly Savalas cared one iota at always being hailed by a constant non-stop stream of passers-by as "Columbo" and "Kojak," respectively. I noticed, when asked for an autograph, each obligingly wrote his famous character name followed by his own.

Fame is fleeting and comes to a precious few, so both Peter and Telly were very comfortable in being recognized, even if they seemed to be known to one and all by the fictitious TV personas that put them constantly in the living rooms of the world. Each was totally content in his own skin and showed no frustration at never having been asked to play Hamlet.

Not all actors felt this way, believe me.

*   *   *

One of my duties as an assistant publicity director for Universal in New York was often to host the press and/or private showings of new films in our screening room high up in the company building. One particular night we had Donald Sutherland and some of his invited guests in to see his latest film. Following the screening, the usual drinks and canapés followed, and they all duly took the elevators down the many floors to the street level. I followed immediately after the last of them departed. This happened literally some ten or fifteen minutes before the big blackout, when all of Manhattan went dark due to a massive historic power failure. I often pondered what I would have done if all the chaos happened a quarter-hour earlier with Sutherland and his group trapped in an elevator and me still up on the screening room floor helpless and in utter darkness. That was one problem that I would not have been able to solve. No matter the circumstances, somehow, in some way, it would have all been the fault of the publicity person *in situ*!

Any man or woman who ever chose this profession will now give a sympathetic smile at reading this truism. My brothers and sisters in arms are on a never-ending tightrope with only one direction to fall. The old amateur and army radio exit line says it all—"Over and Out!"

* * *

My final Bond "activity" took place on the lovely island of Mallorca, where its film commission was giving a major tribute celebrating the career

At director Guy Hamilton's memorial service in Mallorca, Spain, June 2017. From left, unidentified local dignitary, Bond producers Michael G. Wilson and Barbara Broccoli, me, the still lovely Britt Ekland, Frank and Esther Hamilton (Guy's stepson and wife), and members of the local arts community (courtesy Anders Frejdh/From Sweden with Love).

of director Guy Hamilton. The late filmmaker had been a longtime resident. Michael Wilson and Barbara Broccoli most kindly invited me over to join them, Michael's wife, Jane, and Britt Ekland, star of Guy's last of four directorial 007 adventures, *The Man with the Golden Gun*. For many Bond fans, Hamilton's *Goldfinger* is far and away the best Bond ever. It certainly set a pattern for what was to follow. Personally, I am equally impressed by Guy's credits as a first assistant director of three of the greatest motion pictures ever: *The Third Man, The African Queen*, and *The Fallen Idol*.

At the gala dinner following the presentation, I sat between Barbara and Britt, the latter now most friendly. Opposite was Joseph Fiennes, who gained stardom as *Shakespeare in Love*. What a pleasant and cultured personality. While we were conversing, my thoughts went to the title of the early seventies Peter Bogdanovich hit *The Last Picture Show*. Mr. Fiennes was not to know that for me, and for this, he was to be uniquely placed as "the last movie star."

All these words of fame by association can only end by my noting someone I met in Brazil who was famous worldwide while being absolutely unknown! The publicity director there for UA was also a major figure at one of the giant samba schools that compete each year in the annual *Carnival* that takes place before Lent, so he really knew "everyone who is anyone" in Rio.

We were having lunch in one of the street side restaurants just off Copacabana, when this late twenty-something Latin lady walked by, stopped, and gave a warm embrace to my UA colleague. I was introduced, but it all meant nothing until she left. I was then told that this now rather heavyset Carioca had, but a few years earlier, been the muse and inspiration for Antonio Carlos Jobim's hit song that musically swept the recording world. She was no less than the mythical "Girl from Ipanema." As I looked at her rather large posterior receding in the distance, I couldn't help but reflect on another tune, "The Song Has Ended but the Melody Lingers On."

* * *

I have had a great life, and most of my memories are good ones. I loved what I did, and with rare exception wouldn't want to change a thing. The highs far outweigh the lows and my comments (even the negative) are only meant to shine a faint light on what I consider to be of possible interest. My commentary is but one person's observations, not earth-shattering revelations.

In the casbah: Relaxing in a Moroccan-themed room in my house, Valencia, Spain, early 2000s (author's collection).

My own favorite, most "far out" encounter? A good question—I once danced with Ginger Rogers!

Years ago, I was in a poker game and someone won a pot with two pairs—aces and eights. This was the well-known "Dead Man's Hand," held by the famed gunfighter, Wild Bill Hickok, when he was shot and killed at the table in some saloon in the old West. The conversation turned somewhat dark, and we were suddenly discussing what we wanted as our epitaphs when our time came to cash in our chips.

The few words I came up with on that long-ago evening are equally fitting as a closing commentary "End" to these rambling reminisces of a somewhat eventful and unusual life...

"It wasn't dull!"

Index

Numbers in *bold italics* indicate pages with illustrations

215

Index

Index

Index

221

Index